G000244694

Fundsmith Equity Fund, T Class, Acc, inception to 30.10.15

About the Author

Terry Smith graduated in History from University College Cardiff in 1974. He worked for Barclays Bank from 1974 to 1983 and became an Associate of the Chartered Institute of Bankers in 1976. He obtained an MBA at The Management College, Henley in 1979.

He became a stockbroker with W. Greenwell & Co in 1984 and was the top-rated bank analyst in London from 1984 to 1989. In 1990 he became head of UK Company Research at UBS Phillips & Drew, a position from which he was dismissed in 1992 following the publication of his best-selling book *Accounting for Growth*.

He joined Collins Stewart shortly after, and became a director in 1996. In 2000 he became Chief Executive and led the management buy-out of Collins Stewart, which was floated on the London Stock Exchange five months later. In 2003 Collins Stewart acquired Tullett Liberty and followed this in 2004 with the acquisition of Prebon Group, creating the world's second largest inter-dealer broker. Collins Stewart and Tullett Prebon were demerged in 2006 with Terry remaining CEO of Tullett Prebon until September 2014.

In 2010 he founded Fundsmith where he is CEO and CIO. In 2012 he was appointed a Member of the New Zealand Order of Merit for services to New Zealand–UK relations following the success of his campaign to commemorate the New Zealander, Air Marshal Sir Keith Park.

Fundsmith

Celebrating five years of investing in decades of success

Anthology of articles 2010–2015

Terry Smith

MCMLIII Publishing

By the same author

Accounting for Growth (Ed. I and II)

Celebrating five years of investing in decades of success
Anthology of articles 2010–2015
© Terry Smith 2015

First published in 2015 by:

MCMLIII Publishing
33 Cavendish Square
London
W1G 0PW

Printed on FSC certified paper and recycled board.

A catalogue reference for this book can be obtained from the British Library.

ISBN 978 0 9935038 0 1

Fundsmith

Contents

Fundsmith

Fundsmith

For Michaela

Fundsmith
Buy good companies
Don't overpay
Do nothing

Fundsmith

Introduction

We have chosen to re-publish this collection of articles which I have written over the past five years in order to mark the fifth anniversary of the founding of Fundsmith.

When we started the Fundsmith Equity Fund, it was with the aim of providing the best fund you could invest in with the highest return adjusted for risk. How have we fared?

- After five years, the Fund (the T Class Accumulation shares in which I invest, hence the "T") is up by 121% versus 60% for the MSCI World Index in sterling with dividends reinvested (to make it truly comparable with that class of our Fund).

- Our Fund is in the Investment Association's Global Growth Sector which comprises 203 funds. Ours is the 3rd best performing fund over these five years. You might think that means that we have failed in our objective of offering the best return available subject to risk, and frankly your judgement is the one which matters most. However, I would just point out that the two funds which rank ahead of us are specialist healthcare funds. They have performed well in a period which has seen a boom in M&A activity in biotech companies in particular. Their concentration on a single sector is a risk we would not be willing to take and if or when that sector's popularity wanes, so will their performance. Of course, they may then be replaced at the top of the table by another set of sector-specialist funds, and you could have a good performance if you were able to switch between these specialist funds, buying and selling them at an appropriate time. I can only wish you good luck with that approach. It strikes me as analogous to saying you could win a marathon by arranging for it to be run by a team of 100 sprinters each running about 400 metres. To make the analogy accurate, you would have to start the marathon with your first sprinter without knowing whom the other 99 will be and relying upon selecting and recruiting them for each stage at the moment when you needed the baton to be passed on to them. What could possibly go wrong with such an approach? Having deft timing to enable you to change sectors or sector funds every few years has similar demands and risks.

However, this anthology is about the ideas behind our investment strategy rather than the outcome.

As you will hopefully know if you are invested in our Fund, have read any of our materials or attended one of our presentations, we have a simple three-step investment strategy:

1. Only invest in high-quality companies

2. Try not to overpay for their shares

And then

3. Do nothing

I am constantly amazed at the number of people who talk about investment and spend most or all of their time talking about asset allocation, regional allocation, sector weightings, economic forecasts, bonds v equities, interest rates, currencies, risk controls and never mention any need to invest in something good. I naively supposed that the experience of the financial crisis might have taught investors a lesson about the inability to generate good returns from bad assets. No amount of structuring using CDOs,

CLOs, CDOs squared and all the other alphabet soup of structured finance could turn sub-prime loans into investable assets. When things went wrong, even the triple A tranches of those sub-prime loan structures turned out to be triple Z. There's an old saying about silk purses and sow's ears which encapsulates this.

Similarly, it is hard to make a good return over the long term by investing in poor-quality businesses as you are continually faced with the problems of timing and the headwind of their value destruction. If investors have any coherent reason for such investments, they usually are a) diversification and/or b) the belief that they can buy them when their fortunes and share prices are depressed and about to improve and sell them close to or preferably just before they turn down.

Taking the diversification point first, I am also surprised how many investors assume that it is better to be diversified across low-quality investments than to be concentrated in high quality ones.

With regard to b), the performance record of the vast majority of active managers would suggest that there are far more who think they can play the investment and business/economic cycle successfully and outperform despite owning stocks in poor-quality companies than can actually do so.

Probably the most amusing reference I have heard to this strategy was the investor who in 2013, when hope of a more normal economic recovery surfaced for a couple of quarters, said "I own too much quality". Now I know what he means insofar as in an economic recovery the sort of stocks we refuse to own such as heavily cyclical companies, highly leveraged businesses, financials and those which are nearly bust tend to perform best. But even so, try explaining to a child that your main concern is that you own too many good things.

At Fundsmith our primary focus is on owning stocks in good-quality businesses. Many things may and no doubt will still go wrong. We may pay too much for them, although we try not to. The share prices may go down as a result of events beyond our ability to predict. However, whatever may happen, we have the comfort of knowing that our business will over long periods of time sustain and increase their value. If you own poor-quality businesses at difficult times, I am not sure what would comfort you beyond the knowledge that the vast majority of other investors are in the same unenviable position, but then the herd instinct has never been strong in me.

On the subject of valuations, another trait which I find questionable is the obsession with owning "cheap" shares. I have been asked whether a share is cheap many more times than I have been asked whether the company concerned is a good business. Please don't gain the impression that valuation is an inconsequential matter to us. In fact, it is the second leg of our three-part strategy. But we think that you should first decide whether a company is one you would like to own before you even start to consider whether its shares are cheap or expensive.

Moreover, if you are a long-term investor, and in the end which of us isn't, then whether a company is a good business which creates value is a far bigger determinant of the returns you will achieve than the price you pay for it. I covered this subject in the article "Bond proxies: can you afford not to own them?" in the *Financial Times* on 26th June 2015 which is included in this collection and I make no apology for reinforcing the message in this Introduction. That article contained quotes on the subject from Warren Buffett and his business partner Charlie Munger. Buffett's quote was typical insofar as it neatly encapsulated the idea when he said "It's far better to buy a wonderful company at a fair price than a fair company at a wonderful price." There are tens of billions of reasons to believe he's right.

I thought I would also take this opportunity to try to dispel some misconceptions about our investment strategy.

"You try to pick winners" we are often told. No we don't. The companies we invest in have already won. Investors who try to pick winners are those who invest in early-stage technology companies and start-ups, for example. The average company in which we invest started in business over a century ago, as our ad for our fifth anniversary demonstrates (see final page). They have won in the sense that they are dominant market leaders in many or all of their products. Take Colgate-Palmolive. It is the worldwide №1 in toothpaste and toothbrushes. It is also №1 in liquid soap and №2 in soap bars (clearly some work to do). Having identified that these dominant market positions are capable of delivering above-average financial returns we wait, sometimes forever, until the market offers shares in these companies at a valuation which does not fully reflect that they have won. Those of you who like factoids to illustrate a point may be interested to know that when Colgate started paying a dividend, Queen Victoria was on the throne.

"You buy non-cyclical stocks." I have been in work for over 40 years in the financial markets and I have yet to find a truly non-cyclical business. In my view, there is an element of cyclicality in all businesses. Our aim is to find businesses still making good returns on their capital at the bottom of the economic cycle.

"You buy brands." We are interested in consumer goods companies, or more particularly in companies which make Fast-Moving Consumer Goods. We don't like companies which make consumer durables, which are also frequently branded. The ability of the consumer to prolong the life of a durable good if necessary is what makes the performance of these companies too cyclical for us. But we are also interested in medical equipment companies; companies which supply equipment or software from which they generate recurrent revenues from subscriptions, updates, service, spares or consumables; and franchisors.

There are many sectors we will not invest in: financials (banks, insurance and real estate), heavily cyclical businesses (chemicals, steel, engineering and construction), resources (mining and oil and gas), utilities and airlines. We are often confronted by investors who work in or have made fortunes in these sectors and question why we will not invest in them as they made their fortune in them. The answer lies partly in the fact that they made their fortunes because of their individual skill and were entrepreneurial owners or controlling shareholders. Our Fund, on the other hand,

Fundsmith

is in the position of a minority investor in the companies whose stocks we own. We do not control or manage the companies in our portfolio, which is just as well. The other critique we hear of our refusal to invest in these sectors is that "someone must or we will have no airlines/banks/mines". I agree, it just won't be us. We are engaged in trying to maximise long-term returns for our investors rather than an attempt to ensure that funding is available for a wide range of industries, some of which make poor returns.

I would be hard pressed to name the least understood subject in investment given the wide choice available, but I suspect that currencies is amongst the leaders. Lots of people talk or ask about the impact of currencies in a manner which betrays a complete lack of understanding of the subject. The commonest question or assumption about our Fund is the impact of the US dollar since the majority of the companies we have owned since inception are headquartered and listed in America. This makes little or no sense. A company's currency exposure is not determined by where it is headquartered, listed or which currency it denominates its accounts in. Yet this does not seem to stop people assuming that it does and making statements about the exposure of our Fund to the US dollar based upon where the companies are listed.

We own one company which is headquartered and listed in the United States but which has no revenues there at all. Clearly this assumption would not work very well for that company, any more than it would work for the UK-listed company we own which has the United States as its biggest market and which perhaps unsurprisingly reports its accounts in US dollars.

Nor could we understand the reasoning of the commentators who wrote that our holding in Nestlé had benefited from the rise in the Swiss franc. How? 98% of Nestlé's revenues are outside Switzerland. It may be headquartered and listed in Switzerland and report in Swiss francs but the fact is that a company's currency exposure is mainly determined by where it does business. In Nestlé's case, the Indian rupee is a bigger exposure than the Swiss franc.

There is also the point that people seem to have very short-term memories and get obsessed about recent market movements, although this is not limited to currencies. So you will have heard a great deal about the strength of the dollar and we are continually asked about how much benefit our Fund has derived from that when in fact the $/£ cable rate (which is probably the most significant exchange rate for us as we report in pounds and the US dollar is the largest currency exposure for our companies) today is within 6% of where it was on the day our Fund opened in 2010. Big deal.

I have written and spoken so much about market timing that there seems little to add. Market timing is the belief that you can identify tops and bottoms in markets, sectors and companies and take advantage of them by dealing on them or close to them. As you may know, my view is that there are only two sorts of people: those who can't do market timing and those who don't know they can't do it. We are in the former camp. Looking back over five years of our Fund, there are many anecdotes to illustrate this but perhaps my favourite is the investor who declined to invest with us in

December 2010, two months after we opened, as the Fund was up 6% which he regarded as too much. So he decided to wait for it to drop below that level. He is still waiting.

And finally, I am often asked what our investment time horizon is and how long I and my colleagues at Fundsmith intend to run our Fund. My answer is to quote that well-known sage. Not Warren Buffett on this occasion but Buzz Lightyear.

Terry Smith
November 2015

Foreword by Jeff Randall

Terry Smith first caught my eye in 1987 when he was an analyst covering banks at the stockbroker BZW and I was a City reporter on *The Sunday Telegraph*.

Terry had just advised his firm's clients with shares in Barclays to sell them, not a particularly newsworthy event except for the fact that the bank owned BZW.

It occurred to me that this fellow Smith was either an attention-seeking lunatic or a straight-shooting thinker. Either way, he seemed likely to be the source of more good stories – and so it proved.

Barclays' directors were furious and let it be known that if Terry hoped to prosper in the Square Mile, he should find another berth. When Barclays later launched what was in effect a rescue rights issue and passed its dividend, Smith was vindicated.

Come 1992, Terry and I had both moved on. He was head of UK company research at UBS Phillips & Drew and I was City editor of *The Sunday Times.* We met to discuss his new book, *Accounting for Growth*, which shone a light on the chicanery used by some corporate giants to overstate profits.

What surprised me was not that creative accountants had found ways to keep debt off balance sheets, report profits without corresponding cash flow and hide costs. No, the real shocker was that so many household names with lofty reputations were perilously close to cooking the books. Terry's list included Tiphook, Queens Moat Houses, Ratners, Trafalgar House and Maxwell Communications (all long gone).

Some of UBS's clients who had been fingered by Terry kicked up a fuss. In a display of egregious pusillanimity, the bank sacked him. UBS's discomfort soon became embarrassment and then humiliation as many of the companies identified by Smith began to unravel and in some cases collapse amid scandal and government inquiries. From that moment, I decided that Terry was someone worth listening to. Not because he gave us racy headlines, though he certainly did that, but because his research was unusually thorough and his analysis impervious to boardroom pressure.

Unlike many investment managers, Terry is neither a mathematician nor an economist. By education, he is a historian with a rare grasp of common sense. While some others in the investment jungle are looking for new paradigms, Terry is happy to rely on simple precepts that have stood the test of time.

For would-be investors, uncertain about risking money in the stock market, this collection of Terry's newspaper columns is a good place to start. Of course, he does not always get it right. But his essays are readable, easy to digest and refreshingly light on techno-babble. They will help you understand why some companies have durability while others, ostensibly doing well, suddenly disintegrate.

Chapter 1

2010–2011

Make your fund manager walk the plank.

Is your Fund Manager saying yes to yachts while you're deliberating over dinghies?

At Fundsmith, we're focused on careful, disciplined, long-term investment, the kind which isn't compromised by shortcuts and where extortionate fees never have and never will exist. It's for all these reasons why we've invested £25 million of our own money in this one simple fund that comprises only high quality, resilient, global growth companies.

This isn't a new way of investing; it's simply the right way.
It's fund management as it should be.

Fundsmith
www.fundsmith.co.uk

Fund management fees

Straight Talking, 28 September 2010

There has been some recent press about the launch of Fundsmith, my new fund management venture.

Since the press was generated by a leak, there has been much speculation about what features Fundsmith will offer investors. One area of focus of this has been on fees.

Without confirming or denying that fees will be a main area of focus for Fundsmith (we'd like to keep at least some secrets back for the launch), I thought it might provide a flavour of things to come if I comment on some problems with the structure of fees (and costs) which investors in funds currently experience.

RDR

A lot has been written about fund management fees recently, particularly with regard to the impact of the Retail Distribution Review ("RDR"). This comes into effect at the end of 2012 and will thereafter prevent advisers (IFAs, wealth managers and private client stockbrokers) from obtaining payment of part of the egregious upfront fees of up to 5% of the sum invested charged by many fund managers and/or "trail" commission paid from the annual charges levied by managers.

From 2012, advisers will need to obtain payment via advisory fees charged direct to the clients, which may prove somewhat harder to justify when they are explicitly charged to the client rather than paid by the fund manager after he/she has extracted them from the client's investment.

What few people seem to realise is that trail commissions will still be paid to advisers on investments in funds made by clients in 2012 and earlier. This presents an obvious problem. We are told ("Serious Money: Take my (free) advice and avoid a haymaking IFA" by Alice Ross, *Financial Times*, 27th August 2010) that the FSA is monitoring turnover in fund holdings to try to spot any "churning" which may be caused prior to the end of 2012 by advisers getting their clients to invest in funds which will still pay a trail thereafter.

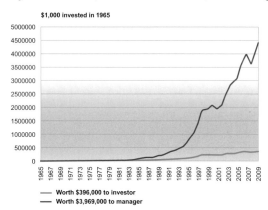

$1,000 invested in 1965

— Worth $396,000 to investor
— Worth $3,969,000 to manager

This leaves a rather more pernicious danger which needs to be watched for: the absence of turnover in those funds after 2012. Whilst activity is something which is correctly seen as the enemy of a good investment performance, it would be unsurprising if, having got their clients into trail-paying funds prior to 2013, a lot of advisers weren't suddenly seized by inactivity. This needs to be guarded against as much as churning.

Two and twenty

Two and twenty is the standard fee formula for the hedge fund industry.

It is unsupportable.

I am not so much shocked as flabbergasted by the number of people who do not realise the impact of these performance fee structures. I am not talking here about the fact that such a performance fee structure clearly led many fund managers to gear up their funds as much as the credit bubble allowed and place bets which many attendees at Las Vegas would regard as outrageous, knowing that they had little or no downside and 20%+ of the upside.

I have had discussions with numerous professionals in sophisticated jobs in the investment industry who are either unaware of or disbelieve the mathematics of what I am about to demonstrate.

As you are aware, Warren Buffett has produced a stellar investment performance over the past 45 years, compounding returns at 20.46% p.a. If you had invested $1,000 in the shares of Berkshire Hathaway when Buffett began running it in 1965, by the end of 2009 your investment would have been worth $4.3m.

However, if instead of running Berkshire Hathaway as a company in which he co-invests with you, Buffett had set it up as a hedge fund and charged 2% of the value of the funds as an annual fee plus 20% of any gains, of that $4.3m, $4.0m would belong to him as manager and only $300,000 would belong to you, the investor. And this is the result you would get if your hedge fund manager had equalled Warren Buffett's performance. Believe me, he or she won't.

Two and twenty does not work. That does not mean that 1.5% and 15% is OK, or even 1% and 10%. Performance fees do not work.

They extract too much of the return and encourage risky behaviour. The only way to focus your fund manager on performance without gifting him or her most of your returns is to ensure he or she invests a major portion of their net worth alongside you in the fund and on exactly the same terms.

TERs and costs

There is a justified focus on the Total Expense Ratio ("TER") of funds which include those expenses which the manager charges to the fund rather than simply on the fund management fee. However, there is one major cost that is not charged to the funds: the cost of dealing in the underlying investments.

This is not insignificant given that, according to FSA research, the average fund manager in the UK turns over their fund 80% per annum. This adds three layers of additional costs: 1. The commissions charged by brokers and investment banks for dealing; 2. The difference between the bid-offer spread for securities sold and bought; and 3. The fact that no fund manager has sufficient good investment ideas to warrant buying and selling 80% of your investment portfolio per annum.

Soon we shall see what Fundsmith can do about all this...

Share buybacks – friend or foe?

Investment Week, **11 April 2011**

Almost 20 years on from publishing my book, *Accounting for Growth*, I am exposing another loophole in the accountancy rules which is allowing companies to appear to have created value when they have not.

Today I am publishing a paper scrutinising the in vogue use of share buybacks – are they a friend or foe to shareholders? Do they create or destroy value?

You might think the answer is obvious, but think again. The problem is when a company repurchases shares they disappear from the balance sheet and this can be used to distort measures of company performance.

Simply by executing a share buyback rather than paying out dividends, companies can inflate their earnings per share (EPS) and are almost universally seen to have created value for shareholders when mostly they clearly have not.

Capital allocation decisions are amongst the most important decisions which management of companies make on behalf of shareholders. Yet share buybacks are not sufficiently understood by company investors and commentators, and maybe even by company management.

One of the most important facts that is continually overlooked is share buybacks only create value if the shares repurchased are trading below intrinsic value and there is no better use for the cash which would generate a higher return.

Most share buybacks destroy value for remaining shareholders, and management is able to get away with this as the current accounting for share buybacks conceals their true effect. So what needs to change?

1. Management should be required to justify share buybacks by reference to the price paid and the implied return and compare this with alternative uses for the cash.

2. Investors and commentators should analyse share buybacks on exactly the same basis as they would if the company bought shares in another company.

3. Investors and commentators should use return on equity to analyse the effect of share buybacks rather than movements in earnings per share.

4. Share buybacks need to be viewed with more than average scepticism when done by companies whose management are incentivised by growth in EPS.

5. Accounting for share buybacks should be changed so that the shares remain as part of shareholders' funds and as an equity accounted asset on the balance sheet in calculating returns.

Exchange-traded funds are worse than I thought

The Telegraph, **24 May 2011**

On 11ᵗʰ January I published my first annual letter to the holders of the Fundsmith Equity Fund. In it, I levelled some criticisms at the investment fad for exchange-traded funds ("ETFs").

One of my basic concerns was that I thought there was a danger of ETFs being mis-sold.

I suspect a lot of retail investors think that ETFs are the same as index funds. Some of them are, but many aren't. In particular, the performance of short ETFs and leveraged ETFs may diverge markedly from what an investor who believes they are simply index funds would expect.

It isn't hard to give examples in which investors would lose money on a leveraged long ETF if the market went up over a period of significant volatility, or in which they lost money owning a short ETF and the market went down over a period in which there were some sharp rallies.

The problem is with the daily compounding of ETFs.

Plus, many ETFs do not contain a basket of the underlying securities or assets which they are attempting to track. Instead, they hold asset swap agreements with a counterparty (often the bank which is the ETF sponsor) which aim to replicate the performance of the index or asset concerned.

There are obvious dangers in such an arrangement in the areas of counterparty risk and collateralisation of the sort which caused so many problems during the Credit Crisis.

A good example of the potential risks here is given by PEK, the NYSE-listed Market Vectors China A Shares ETF. It is illegal for foreign investors other than licensed institutions to buy A Shares listed in Shanghai or Shenzhen. So the ETF owns swaps with brokers who are licensed to hold the underlying shares. If PEK owned a significant portion of the float in A Shares and its holders tried to liquidate at speed, it might be interesting.

Some commentators claim we need not worry much about retail investors misunderstanding ETFs as in Europe at least, they are mainly utilised by institutional investors.

This of course misses a couple of vital points. One is that the underlying clients for many of those "institutions" are individual investors – do they really understand the risks their private wealth manager is running with ETFs?

Also, the *Financial Times* FTfm supplement carried an article on 9th May pointing out this lack of direct retail involvement in ETFs in Europe on the same day as the wrap-around advert for its supplement was supplied by Amundi ETF. On that day, commuters coming into London were being given handouts of glossy brochures on Amundi ETFs plus a natty plastic credit card/season ticket wallet emblazoned with the slogan:

"Amundi ETF: More than just another tracker."

Quite so.

At this rate, we may soon have to worry about the direct retail involvement in ETFs.

However, there is another and perhaps more pernicious danger with ETFs than misunderstanding or mis-selling.

An ETF is in effect a hybrid vehicle which combines features of an open-ended or mutual fund with those of a closed-end fund. They are like open-ended funds insofar as a purchaser buys or redeems so-called creation units. But they are also tradable in the secondary market, so ostensibly providing real-time liquidity.

Secondary trading activity brings with it the possibility that market participants will short the ETFs themselves. And there is no limit to the short selling, which is impossible in an ETF in the same way that there is in an equity.

In an ordinary equity, the short selling is limited by the ability of the short sellers to borrow the stock so that they can deliver it to complete their sell bargains. In an ETF, a short seller can always rely on the process of creating shares in the ETF to ensure he can deliver. This leads to the possibility that a buyer of an ETF share is buying for a short seller and that no new share has yet been created.

The investors who buy from the short sellers don't own a claim on the underlying basket of securities or swap in the ETF; they own a promise to deliver the ETF share given by the short seller.

The problem this causes is that as no new shares are created in the ETF by this process, the assets of the ETF may become significantly less than the outstanding cumulative buy orders would suggest. This is a significant problem given reports that there has been short selling up to levels of 1000pc short in some ETFs.

You might think that one way to overcome the risks involved in this at a stroke is for the ETF sponsor to create the shares represented by the cumulative buying interest, but this may be easier said than done.

Take an ETF like IWM in which the short interest recently exceeded 100pc or $15bn (£9.3bn). IWM invests in the Russell 2000 US Small Cap Index. To invest $15bn in the basket of stocks involved would require about a week's trading – and that is if the ETF creation was the sole trading in those stocks. The scope for a short squeeze is tremendous.

The net result is that across the entire ETF asset class portion of the funds which ETF purchasers think have been invested in ETFs, via the creation of new shares, has in effect been lent to hedge funds. The ETF holdings are not all backed by assets of the sort investors expect, even if they understand what the ETF is meant to do.

Perhaps these little understood structural issues explain why 70pc of the cancelled trades in last May's Flash Crash were in ETFs when ETFs represent only 11pc of the securities in issue in the US.

Moreover, in the case of some ETFs such as PEK, it is difficult to fathom what the short interest in PEK really represents as it is illegal to short China A shares.

Another example of the issues in this sector which recently crossed my desk was a fundraising proposition for a business which undertakes trading in ETFs. It shall of course remain nameless, but it trades, arbitrages and makes prices in ETFs with a particular focus on the less traded ETFs. This company describes itself as a "fairly thinly capitalised entity". There are echoes of the parallel banking system in the Credit Crisis here.

It also describes the pace of development in the ETF area as "breakneck". I just wonder whose neck will eventually get broken.

Murdoch should give up control of News Corp

Investment Week, **13 July 2011**

The announcement of an increased share buyback at News Corporation is clearly meant as a sop to shareholders who might justifiably be querying whether Murdoch family control is really in their best interests.

The main criteria which determine whether a share buyback creates value for remaining shareholders are a) the shares should be trading below intrinsic value; and b) there should be no better alternative use for the cash that would deliver better returns than the buyback.

Given the outcome of News Corp's acquisitive activity in recent years, there seems little doubt a buyback would deliver better value than, for example, the acquisition of MySpace, for which News Corp paid $580m and then sold it for $35m, or the acquisition of Dow Jones for $5.7bn which has so far produced a $2.8bn write-down.

Whether or not News Corp's shares are cheap is more difficult to determine. They are certainly low-rated relative to peers such as Disney, Time Warner or Viacom, but the fundamental prospects must be more than usually difficult to determine in the light of the phone-hacking scandal and the uncertainty this has caused over the future of Sky.

More generally, looking at the performance of News Corp, an investor should surely query why Rupert Murdoch believes the best person to control News Corp must be someone named Murdoch.

So far his clan's control has produced a mediocre 10% return on capital employed over the past five years, and a share price which has underperformed the S&P 500 index for the past 15 years.

It is almost certain that what would create far more value than a buyback would be for News Corp to enfranchise the Class A non-voting shares which the Murdoch family does not own.

News Corp: a family business

The Guardian, **18 July 2011**

Last week while I was in New York, I had the unusual experience of being interviewed about the implications of the phone-hacking scandal in the newsroom of Fox News for Sky TV. So I was being interviewed in the epicentre of Rupert Murdoch's news empire in America for the satellite TV channel where his son James is chairman and in which, at least until last week, his News Corp master vehicle was trying to buy out the outside shareholders. What happened in the interview was revealing about some aspects of this scandal which have yet to come into full focus.

In my view, the Sky News interviewer, Anna Jones, demonstrated a pro-Murdoch bias. I suggested to her that, as the CEO of a public company, I think the shareholders would have had me fired if I had indulged in the following:

1. Paid $580m (£360m) for MySpace and then sold it for $35m (£22m);

2. Paid $5.7bn (£3.5bn) for Dow Jones and written off $2.8bn (£1.7bn);

3. Paid $615m (£382m) for my daughter's business in an example of what has been described as "blatant nepotism";

4. Seen my company's shares underperform the S&P 500 Index for 15 years; and

5. Been in charge when several of my staff had engaged in criminal phone hacking and bribing police officers, activities which had been covered up by my management.

So, I asked, why hasn't Murdoch been fired? The answer, of course, is that nobody can fire Rupert Murdoch because the Murdochs control News Corp through differential voting rights.

News Corp has two classes of share capital: A shares which carry no votes, and B shares which have all the votes. The Murdochs own 40% of the B voting shares. The much more numerous A shares have no votes, so the Murdochs are able to control a company in which they own only 13% of the total issued share capital being the total of the A and B shares.

So when News Corp paid $615m for Elisabeth Murdoch's business, Shine, her father was literally buying it mainly with other people's money – which as we all know is much easier to spend than your own. Similarly, the impact in terms of lost value of the other disasters which I mentioned has mainly fallen on those long-suffering but non-voting A shareholders in News Corp because they are putting up most of the money.

My responses about the Murdoch situation were clearly not what the Sky interviewer was expecting, or wanted to hear. She mounted a defence of Rupert Murdoch's achievements in building a "big empire". I reminded her that to qualify as a business empire, News Corp would need to generate, for example, a decent return on capital – something which it has failed to do.

Return on capital employed is one of the most important measures of corporate performance – it is the profit return which the management earns on the capital shareholders provide. News Corp has managed a decidedly poor return on capital employed of just 10% a year in the past five years. Comparable companies have done much better: the US media company Viacom managed a return of 20% a year and Daily Mail and General Trust 30% a year.

The interviewer ended by cutting me off after she said she would like to take me through the achievements of James Murdoch and Elisabeth Murdoch. I would welcome that debate on live TV. Of course, the clip of the interview on the Sky website omits the interviewer's questions and comments.

If this is the standard of editorial independence and integrity at Sky before the Murdochs owned the company outright, one can only cringe at the thought of what would have followed if they gained outright ownership.

The whole litany of phone hacking, police bribery, and cosiness with politicians of both major parties who competed to see who could engage in the greatest pandering to the Murdoch acolytes is, in general terms, an example of an abuse of power. So is the shareholder voting structure at News Corp.

News International published an apology in the newspapers for the phone-hacking scandal. Rupert Murdoch should apologise in person to his shareholders for the damage he has wrought and, since actions speak louder than words, he should enfranchise the class A non-voting shares which the Murdoch family does not own. Then the owners of News Corp can pass judgment upon his actions.

UBS debacle highlights dangers of ETFs

Investment Week, **16 September 2011**

The losses of $2bn incurred by an allegedly rogue trader on the Delta One desk at UBS have again raised the subject of the (lack of) risk controls by banks dealing in opaque instruments, the need to separate investment and retail banking and the risks inherent in ETFs.

I have written over the past year about the unappreciated risks in ETFs and it is probably time to bring these thoughts up to date. ETFs are regarded by many investors as the same as index funds.

They clearly are not:

1. Some ETFs do not hold physical assets of the sort they seek to track. They are "synthetic" and hold derivatives. This gives rise to a counterparty risk, and as we saw with the UBS incident, some interesting risks within the counterparties supplying the basket of derivatives.

   What if (when?) such ETF trades cause such a mammoth loss in a counterparty which does not have sufficient capital to bear the loss and pay out under the derivative contract? Answer: the ETF will fail.

2. ETFs do NOT always match the underlying in the way people expect. Because of daily rebalancing and compounding, you can own a leveraged long ETF and lose money over a period when the market goes up but during which there are some sharp falls.

   Equally, you can own an inverse ETF (which provides a short exposure) during a period when the market goes down but there are some sharp rallies and lose money. This actually occurred with some inverse ETFs in 2008. I would strongly suggest that people would not expect to be leveraged long and lose money if the market goes up or short and lose it when it goes down.

3. Because you can exchange trade these funds, they are used by hedge funds and banks to take positions and they can short them. Because they can apparently rely upon creating the units to deliver on their short, there are examples of short interest in ETFs being up to 1000% short, i.e. some market participants are short 10 times the amount of the ETF.

If the ETF is in an illiquid sector, can you really rely upon creating the units as you may not be able to buy (or sell) the underlying assets in a sector with limited liquidity?

In the past week, I am told there have been examples of the cost of borrowing (the cost of borrowing stock to deliver on a short sale until such time as you close the short by buying back) up to 14% p.a. on the IWM ETF (the iShares Russell 2000 Index ETF). Now why would someone pay 14% p.a. to borrow something in what is more or less a zero interest rate environment and when you should be able to deliver the underlying securities to create unlimited units in the ETF?

The answer, I suspect, is that the short sellers cannot create the units because the ETF operates in an area with limited liquidity (the Russell 2000 is the US Small Cap Stock Index).

The dangers of allowing short sales which are a multiple of the value of a fund in an area where it may not be possible to close the trades by buying back the stocks are clear, but amazingly, during the debate in which I have been engaged by various cheerleaders for ETFs, they have claimed there is no such risk in shorting ETFs. They clearly do not understand the product they are peddling, and if they can't, what chance has the retail investor got?

4. Although ETFs are billed as low cost, they are also the most profitable asset management product for a number of providers. How can this apparent contradiction be so? The answer is that the charge for managing the ETF is only one part of the cost.

There are also the hidden costs in the synthetic and derivative trades which the provider undertakes for the ETF. As a result of all this, I have long thought and written that there is a certainty that ETFs are being mis-sold to the retail market and that the risks that are being incurred in running, constructing, trading and holding them are not sufficiently understood. After the UBS incident, I think this should be regarded as indisputable.

Chapter 2

2011–2012

Fundsmith understands the benefits of keeping investment simple.

Past performance is not necessarily a guide to future performance. The value of investments and the income from them may fall as well as rise and be affected by changes in exchange rates, and you may not get back the amount of your original investment. Fundsmith LLP does not offer investment advice or make any recommendations regarding the suitability of its product.

An English language prospectus for the Fundsmith Equity Fund is available on request and via the Fundsmith website and investors should consult this document before purchasing shares in the fund. This financial promotion is intended for UK residents only and is communicated by Fundsmith LLP which is authorised and regulated by the Financial Services Authority.

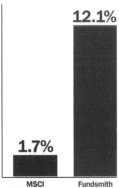

12.1%

1.7%

MSCI World Index   Fundsmith Equity Fund

1st Nov 2010 to 31st Oct 2011
Source: Fundsmith Equity Fund performance is for £ T Class Accumulation shares and is stated net of fees priced at midday GMT time. MSCI World Index is sourced from Bloomberg, is in £, includes income reinvested and is priced at close of business US time.

Traders are the ruin of retail banking

The Guardian, 1 July 2012

The reaction of the British Bankers' Association to the revelation that Barclays traders had been manipulating the Libor interest rates – they say they were "shocked" – is reminiscent of the scene in the movie *Casablanca* in which the gendarme Captain Renault closes down Rick's gambling joint and says "I'm shocked, shocked to find that gambling is going on in here!" while simultaneously pocketing his winnings.

If the BBA was genuinely unaware that manipulation of Libor was going on, then its officers need to get out more. Its assertion looks doubly ridiculous given that it shares a chairman with Barclays, and will look increasingly unbelievable if, as seems likely, more banks are found to have engaged in this practice and other benchmark rates are found to have been rigged.

A great banker, the late Sir Brian Pitman, once said that most banks serve their employees well, but few serve their customers or shareholders. There was never any doubt that he was right about this, as he was about most things. But what conclusions should we draw from this latest example?

First, the arguments against separating retail and investment banks were always thin. Now they are surely unanswerable. It is quite clear that whenever we allow investment bank traders to operate alongside retail bank operations which are central to the economy's essential functions of credit creation and payment systems, the traders will overwhelm the retail bankers and the results will be damaging to the vital retail banking operations. We saw this in the causes of the credit crunch when the investment bankers devised an alphabet soup of toxic products – CDOs, CLOs, CDOs-squared – and sold them to customers of the banks. We have seen it again with the staff taking part in the Libor setting suborned by their traders.

What needs to happen? The UK and the US must enact a Glass–Steagall Act (the 1933 banking act passed in the wake of the Great Crash, which separated commercial and investment banking) and separate retail and investment banks. Ringfencing, as proposed by the Vickers Commission, will not work. As this Libor scandal illustrates, ways will be found to climb over, burrow under and go round the ringfence. The only people who seem to have lobbied against such separation are bankers. Why are we listening to them? Here the government has failed – its natural affinity to business has allowed it to be persuaded by the special pleading of the investment bankers who are now running many of our banks.

Second, we need to repeal those aspects of Big Bang which allowed banks, investment banks and brokerage firms to combine operations in which they traded for their own account and also acted as an agent for clients. In such organisations, the client always loses.

In addition, we need to learn an important lesson about who should be allowed to run banks. Traders should never be allowed to run banks. Traders are all about the short term and their myopia leads them to do things for short-term profit which risk ruination in the longer term. In my view, every bank that puts a trader in charge risks ruin. Take a look at the examples of Salomon Brothers, Bear Stearns and Lehman.

Look back to an era before British banks got into the problems which have followed their adventures in investment banking: their leaders were from a retail banking background – men like Bruce Pattullo and Peter Burt at Bank of Scotland, Willie Purves at HSBC, Malcolm Williamson at Standard Chartered and of course Brian Pitman at Lloyds. Knights of the realm to a man, and there's never been any question of a need to strip them of their honours. They were real bankers, and that's a compliment.

What is the Spanish word for zombie?

Investment Week, 1 October 2012

"El zombi" is Spanish for "zombie". The term "zombie" is used to describe an economy in which failing companies continue to operate with government support. The term traces back to Edward Kane's (The S&L Insurance Mess: How Did It Happen?, 1989) explanation of the situation of insolvent savings and loan associations in the 1980s. But it is most commonly used to describe Japan in the early 1990s.

After Japan's real estate bubble burst at the end of the 1980s, there was a conspiracy aimed at keeping its banks which were bust lending to real estate and other affected companies which were also bust. This simply offended the good rule about not sending good money after bad. It was a misallocation of capital resources, and a society which allows widespread misallocation of its capital is doomed.

In Japan, it postponed the necessary market cycle of creative destruction in which failed enterprises close down and new capital is allocated to viable operators who can make a positive return on it. It was a major contributory factor to Japan's "lost decade" without any economic growth. Think about it this way: would your wealth grow if you kept pumping money into a loss-making investment?

Why do I mention this? Because, according to a report by R.R. de Acuña & Asociados, a property consulting firm, almost half of Spain's 67,000 property developers are insolvent but not bankrupt after getting additional financing from banks. We are seeing Japan

Mk 2 played out in Spain. The bailout of the Spanish banks and no doubt in due course of Spain itself will be for the unstated purpose of funding these zombies with the inevitable, dire consequences.

The headlines at the weekend about Spain were the outcome of the latest stress test which apparently shows that the Spanish banks need an additional €60bn of capital. The credibility of stress tests for eurozone banks have long since been stretched beyond breaking point, but in any event, you have to question the sense in recapitalising zombie banks.

Lessons of the great Wall Street Crash

The Independent, 24 October 2012

The philosopher George Santayana said "Those who do not remember the past are condemned to repeat it." We are in the sixth year of the financial crisis which started in 2007 and experiencing problems which are reminiscent of the Great Depression with faltering economic growth, high unemployment, deflation, and a badly damaged and still shaky banking system.

It's therefore unsurprising that commentators and policy makers would look to that period for lessons on what to do and what to avoid.

However, what we need in order to learn from the Great Depression is a firm grasp of what happened then. Most commentary I hear or read is along the lines of: "The Great Depression was triggered by the Wall Street Crash, itself the result of laissez-faire capitalism. The Depression was deepened as a result of the failure of governments to adopt what would come to be called Keynesian techniques to stimulate demand and by adherence to the Gold Standard. It was only when Franklin D. Roosevelt took office and implemented the New Deal that America began to recover from the Depression as these Keynesian methods stimulated demand."

Sadly, this version of events owes more to myth than reality. Firstly, the idea that laissez-faire free market policies were the root cause of the Crash and subsequent Depression is far removed from reality. In fact, Herbert Hoover, who preceded Roosevelt as President until 1932, was criticised by FDR for "reckless and extravagant spending" and "thinking we ought to control everything in Washington", and he introduced the Smoot–Hawley Tariff in 1930 which stopped many imports. The dramatic contraction of the money supply by the Fed which began in 1929 and the rise in interest rates from 1928 helped to cause and then exacerbate the impact of the Crash. This was not simply a failure of capitalism or free markets. It had a lot of help from the government. The Hoover administration was interventionist, not laissez-faire, and its interventions caused problems and made matters worse.

But surely all this changed after FDR said "We have nothing to fear but fear itself" (which was not original – it was a phrase borrowed from 19th century writer Henry Thoreau)? Roosevelt announced spending of $10bn when government revenues were $3bn a year, and government spending rose by 83 per cent between 1933 and 1936 while federal debt rose by 73 per cent.

Simultaneously, many measures were implemented which were a drag on economic activity. The Social Security Act which introduced a minimum wage kept many unskilled workers out of the labour market. The Agricultural Adjustment Act produced the destruction of crops and cattle. The National Recovery Administration or NRA created a massive bureaucracy which increased the cost of doing business significantly: shortening hours and raising wages. Night work was banned. Five hundred NRA codes were introduced governing production of articles ranging from lingerie to lightning rods. So-called "cut throat" pricing was banned – a tailor was sent to jail for pressing a suit for 35 cents instead of the NRA-mandated

40 cents. How these anti-competitive and bureaucratic measures were supposed to promote activity is a mystery. The net result was industrial production dropped 25 per cent in the six months after the NRA came into effect.

Simultaneously, Roosevelt's Civil Works Administration (CWA) engaged in employment of masses in some perfectly pointless activities such as researching the history of the safety pin and using balloons to frighten birds away from public buildings. When the CWA became the Works Progress Administration (WPA), similar nonsense continued such as cataloguing ways of cooking spinach. In a foretaste of our times, WPA workers were also used to collect Democratic Party campaign contributions. So was born the idea of a "client" class dependent on the state who would automatically vote for the party giving the handouts. The parallel with today's loyal Labour following in the public sector in the North of England, Scotland and Wales is obvious.

Far from ending the Great Depression, such measures served to prolong it – preventing the workforce from seeking real jobs and diverting resources to politically motivated projects.

They were accompanied by a series of anti-business and "soak the rich" tax provisions. The top marginal rate of income tax was raised first to 79 per cent then to 90 per cent, personal tax exemption was lowered to just $600 a year, estate tax went up to 70 per cent and gift tax to 52.5 per cent. Corporate taxes were also raised with surtaxes for undistributed profits.

Unsurprisingly, the economy slumped back into depression in 1938 and the stock market halved again from 1937 to 1938, which can hardly have been the result of laissez-faire capitalism. FDR acolytes claim this was due to the Supreme Court outlawing the NRA and premature attempts to cut spending and balance the budget. But it is estimated that the reduction which resulted from this was only about 1 per cent of GDP which was far too small to cause the problem – just as austerity cannot now be the cause of the UK's problems because there hasn't been any yet. Government spending has continued to rise inexorably since the Coalition took office.

By the time war broke out in 1941, unemployment was still 17 per cent. Hardly a triumph for two presidential terms of Keynesian policies.

So what did pull America out of the Depression? The Second World War? America's involvement in the war was unique. It did not join the war until two years after it started, allowing America to benefit from the rearmament of the Allies as the "arsenal of democracy", to quote FDR. Even when it entered the war, it suffered none of the destruction of assets and infrastructure which the other Allies did, other than the attack on Pearl Harbour, and so had all the benefits in terms of demand from rearmament and none of the disruption suffered by other combatants.

The war was then followed by the Truman administration, which was far less anti-business than FDR's had been. This combination of factors was the cause of recovery.

We have to learn from history if we are not to repeat its mistakes, but we will learn nothing if the experiences of history are heavily edited to suit political agendas and prejudices. We need to be told the truth.

Chapter 3
2012–2013

Are these the only stocks your Fund Manager should be in?

The Fundsmith Equity Fund is a global equity fund launched by Terry Smith to run his own money and that of anyone who wishes to co-invest with him. The fund is a concentrated portfolio of large, global, growing, cash generative companies that we invest in for the long term. Thus portfolio turnover is very low.

Past performance is not necessarily a guide to future performance. The value of investments and the income from them may fall as well as rise and be affected by changes in exchange rates, and you may not get back the amount of your original investment. Fundsmith LLP does not offer investment advice or make any recommendations regarding the suitability of its product.

An English language prospectus, a Key Investor Information Document (KIID) and a Supplementary Information Document (SID) for the Fundsmith Equity Fund are available on request and via the Fundsmith website and investors should consult these documents before purchasing shares in the fund. This financial promotion is intended for UK residents only and is communicated by Fundsmith LLP which is authorised and regulated by the Financial Services Authority.

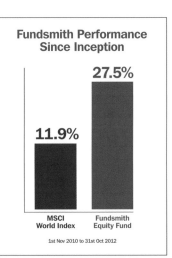

Fundsmith Performance Since Inception

27.5%

11.9%

| MSCI World Index | Fundsmith Equity Fund |

1st Nov 2010 to 31st Oct 2012

% Total Return	1ˢᵗ Nov 2010 to 31ˢᵗ Oct 2011	1ˢᵗ Nov 2011 to 31ˢᵗ Oct 2012
Fundsmith Equity Fund[1]	+12.1	+13.7
MSCI World Index[2]	+1.7	+10.1

Source: Bloomberg [1]T Class Accumulation Shares in GBP, net of fees, priced at midday UK time. [2]In GBP, dividends reinvested, priced at 4pm US EST.

Lessons from the Tour de France

Financial Times, **23 November 2012**

The Tour de France has been in the news a lot this year, with a Brit winning it for the first time and Lance Armstrong being stripped of his titles for alleged doping.

You might ask what this has to do with investment. There's at least one vital lesson for successful investment from the Tour. It will be run for the 100th time next year, yet has never been won by a rider who won every stage, and it never will.

That's because cyclists, like investment products, are built for different ends. Imagine the peloton is like the mass of index-hugging funds. In each stage (quarter or year) it produces a winner, but the leadership continually changes. In the mountain stages, the climbers are those defensive funds that outperform in adverse market conditions, but don't do so well in rampant bull markets. The sprinters are the High Frequency Traders built for speed. Gearing and derivatives are the investment equivalent of EPO and steroids – they can boost performance but at a cost, and added risk.

The Tour has three distinct stages. In the flat stages, the riders group together in the peloton, gaining advantage by slipstreaming those around them to save the effort of riding alone.

In the time trial stages, the riders are on bikes with tri-bars on which they place their arms so that their posture is more aerodynamic. They wear skinsuits because they cannot "slipstream" as in the peloton. They set off individually, so the result is a pure test of riding ability.

Then there are the lung-busting mountain stages in which the rider must ride up alpine passes and roads. Here, it's about endurance.

There is no one rider with the physique to win all three types of stage. The way to win is to be excellent at one discipline, not bad at others, and to work with your team.

Searching for an investment strategy or fund manager who can outperform the market in all reporting periods and varying market conditions is as pointless as trying to find a rider who can win every stage of the Tour. But this is precisely what many investors do. We persist in examining our funds' performance in every reporting period, as often as every quarter, and sometimes exiting when a manager underperforms.

An element of this is sensible – investment performance has to be measured over some time period, and some funds are persistent "dogs" in almost all market conditions.

But a quarter is too short a period to judge performance reasonably, and even a year is just the time it takes the earth to go round the sun. It is not a natural time period over which to measure the performance of any business or investment unless it is linked to the earth's orbit. To assess an investment strategy or a fund, you need to see its results across a full economic cycle with both bull and bear markets.

There is a lot of evidence to suggest that where investors are switching between funds and changing investment strategies, their timing is almost invariably wrong. Professional investors, in the form of trustees of endowments and pension funds, are just as guilty of this as retail investors. They often ditch managers after a poor streak only to find those managers recover their touch, while those they have adopted start to underperform. That would be like Team Sky parting with a cyclist who failed to win a mountain stage, only to see him triumph in a time trial.

Even worse are any strategies which rely upon an element of market timing. As the old saying goes, there are only two types of investor: those who can't time the markets, and those who don't know they can't time the markets. Like the Tour, investment is a test of endurance, and the winner will be the investor who finds a good strategy or fund and sticks with it.

Return-free risk – why boring is best

Financial Times, **18 January 2013**

The title of this piece is a play on the expression "risk-free return" used to describe the return on investment which can be obtained without incurring any risk to the capital sum invested. Prior to the current financial crisis, this characteristic was generally assumed to apply to sovereign debt in the developed world.

The efficient-market hypothesis (EMH) asserts that financial markets are "efficient" in that the only way an investor can achieve higher returns is to take on more risk. But this is not necessarily true in practice. Research by Robert Haugen of Haugen Financial Systems and Nardin Baker of Guggenheim Partners shows that the least volatile decile of stocks generated annualised total returns of 8.7 per cent, while the most volatile decile lost 8.8 per cent a year. These results seem flatly to contradict the risk/return bit of the EMH.

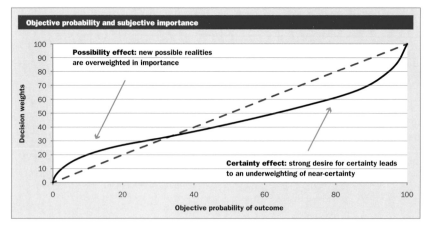

Source: Kahneman (2011)

Another study by Goldman Sachs brings in fundamental quality – defined as cash return on cash invested, or CROCI

It created portfolios based upon CROCI performance and found that market returns increase with relative CROCI. Better companies made better investments.

But why can "quality" shares outperform like this when EMH postulates that only more risk can drive superior returns? Part of the answer lies in investor psychology.

Imagine you have a gravely ill loved one, but you can purchase treatment that would enhance their chances of survival by 10 per cent. What would you pay for it?

Research suggests that this depends upon their starting chances of survival without the treatment. If their chances were 50/50, then a 10 per cent improvement would certainly be valuable.

But if their chances were zero, I'd suggest most people would pay more to improve that to 10 per cent.

Similarly, most people would surely pay more highly for certainty – if the relative had a 90 per cent chance of survival, but by paying you could take this to 100 per cent.

This goes some way towards explaining why investors will buy a bond which yields less than an equity in the same company. They desire certainty of outcome: the bond will pay a certain coupon and be redeemed for a certain value at a certain time. By contrast, dividends from the equity may vary or even disappear and the price of the shares is unpredictable. Daniel Kahneman, the psychologist and behavioural economist, illustrates this point in his book *Thinking, Fast and Slow* using the chart on page 36.

The solid line is the "decision weight" – the psychological importance attached to each level of probability, derived from laboratory experiments. You can see that from about zero to 30 per cent probability of survival, the relative will pay more for a given level of probability. From about 30 per cent to close to 100 per cent they will underpay, but there is a sharp increase in the relative amount they will pay from about 90 per cent probability to certainty.

In investing, the near-certain bit just before 90 per cent is the world of low beta/high-quality stocks. They have bond-like returns and low share price volatility, but they are still stocks with uncertainty about share price and dividend payments.

This helps to explain why "boring" quality stocks tend to be consistently undervalued, and that undervaluation is what helps to produce superior performance.

The upshot of all this is relatively simple, but nonetheless startling. Rather than seeking superior portfolio performance by chasing high-risk stocks ("return-free risk"), investors should seek out "boring" quality companies which have predictable returns and superior fundamental financial performance, and take advantage of their persistent undervaluation relative to those returns to buy and hold them.

Ten golden rules of investment

Financial Times, **15 February 2013**

In theory, individual private investors have plenty of advantages compared to managers of big retail and pension funds. They don't have to write quarterly reports to investors justifying their fees. They don't have to worry about beating benchmarks all the time. And they're not constrained by rules about liquidity or limits on portfolio constituents.

But many investors fail to capitalise fully on these advantages because they make basic mistakes, such as buying the wrong companies, trading too often and paying charges that are too high. My rules are designed to help investors avoid such pitfalls – I'll be expanding on some of them in future columns.

1. **If you don't fully understand it, don't invest**

   Reginald Mitchell, the designer of the iconic Spitfire fighter plane, once said: "If anybody ever tells you anything about an aeroplane which is so bloody complicated you can't understand it, take it from me: it's all balls."

   The same is true in investment. How many investors have bought, or rather been sold, "structured products" without truly understanding the risks involved? My personal favourite to illustrate this point is a fund launched in 2011 by Parkstone Asset Management called The Tracker UK Managed Alpha Fund. This described itself as a "securitised derivative, low-cost, actively managed, multi-asset, structured investment". I wonder what it does.

I always think that if you can't understand what an investment does, it is because you are not meant to understand. So don't invest in it.

2. **Don't try to time the market**

"Market timing" is investing somewhere near the bottom in market cycles and getting out somewhere near the top. It sounds obvious and simple, but in practice it works in reverse: money flows into funds and markets when they have gone up and comes out when they have gone down.

Stocks are a "Giffen good" for most investors – demand paradoxically rises as their price increases. Investors feel comforted by the presence of others investing or dis-investing alongside them, rather like lemmings heading towards a cliff edge together. We don't enjoy the lonely feeling of the contrarian who invests when everyone else is selling and sells when everyone else is bullish.

Humans are hard-wired to be bad at market timing, so don't try to do it.

3. **Minimise fees**

Fees paid to fund managers and advisers are a drag on investment performance. The average UK investor who invests via an adviser, uses a platform and then invests in mutual funds incurs total charges of about 3 per cent each year. This is higher than the yield on equities and most government bonds. So all and more of the income from his or her investments is being consumed by fees.

4. Deal as infrequently as possible

Since we're so bad at market timing, and fees eat into our returns, it logically follows that investors should deal as infrequently as possible. The same applies to fund managers. But the Financial Services Authority estimated that the average UK mutual fund manager turns over 80 per cent of his or her portfolio each year, and in so doing incurs an additional cost of about 1.0–1.4 per cent in commissions, bid/offer spreads and stamp duty. This lot is added to annual management fees and is yet another drag on your investment performance.

5. Don't over-diversify

While portfolio diversification can improve your investment performance, it does have limits and is not without drawbacks. Research suggests that 90 per cent of diversification benefits can be obtained in most markets with a portfolio of just over 20 stocks. The more you diversify beyond that, the less you know about each investment.

6. Never invest just to avoid tax

Instruments like venture capital trusts, enterprise investment schemes and film finance projects are primarily vehicles to enable you to avoid or defer tax. Many investors who put money into them have no burning desire to invest in movies or solar panels. They are so blinded by the tax advantages that they tend to overlook the mammoth fees and the poor performance of the underlying investments. It's often cheaper just to pay the tax.

7. **Never invest in poor-quality companies**

A good company is one that regularly makes a high return in cash terms on capital employed, and can reinvest at least part of that cash flow in order to grow its business and compound the value of your investment. Bad companies do not do this. They make inadequate returns on the capital they employ. You may think you should invest in these poor companies as they are going to improve because the management will change, or they will be taken over, or their results will pick up with the economic or business cycle. But each day you wait for such events, these companies destroy a little bit more value. Good companies do the opposite. With a good company, time is on your side.

8. **Buy shares in a business which can be run by an idiot**

Never buy shares in companies which require a genius or charismatic chief executive to make them work. Sooner or later that individual will no longer be there, and what then?

9. **Don't engage in "greater fool theory"**

Only buy investments that you really want to own and at a price at which you are happy to own them. If you buy shares – or any other investment – with the sole intention of on-selling them, or if you overpay even for good companies, you are engaging in "greater fool theory". The success of that strategy depends upon someone else being willing to play the same game.

10. If you don't like what's happening to your shares, switch off the screen

The price of the shares you buy may vary for reasons which have nothing to do with the fundamentals of the business. So movements in share prices are not necessarily a guide to whether your investment is good or bad. If you have chosen shares in good companies or a fund at reasonable prices, and you find gyrations in their prices unsettling, then simply stop looking at the share price.

Part 1: market timing: don't try this at home

Financial Times, **1 March 2013**

What is meant by market timing? It's the classic investor aim: to buy low and sell high. This can be applied to individual stocks or funds, trying to buy them at the bottom of a business or market cycle and sell close to the top, or to the timing of committing your funds to the market as a whole – waiting for a market bottom before coming out of cash and taking the plunge, and cashing out when the market is at a top.

Nothing wrong with that, you might think. Surely it enhances your return to miss the fall in markets from a peak and get back in for the recovery from its lows? It does indeed. The trouble is that very few, if any of us, are any good at it.

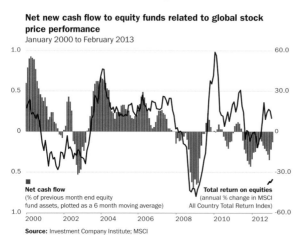

Net new cash flow to equity funds related to global stock price performance
January 2000 to February 2013

■ **Net cash flow**
(% of previous month end equity fund assets, plotted as a 6 month moving average)

Total return on equities
(annual % change in MSCI All Country Total Return Index)

Source: Investment Company Institute; MSCI

There is quite a lot of data available about investors' behaviour and as the chart shows, investors' flows into and out of funds mainly achieve the opposite of what is desired. Money flows into markets and funds when they have risen and flows out when they have fallen – precisely the opposite of what effective market timing would require.

Professional investors, such as fund managers and trustees of pension funds and endowments, may scoff at this as the typical herd instinct of retail investors. But the available evidence suggests that they are no better. The average active fund manager underperforms the market and Cambridge Associates' data clearly shows that the average pension fund or endowment decision to hire or fire a fund manager is just as mistimed.

It is not hard to see why we are almost all bad at market timing. It is hard enough to have the strength of conviction to convince yourself that markets are too high and sell when the background is looking rosy and everyone else is bullish. But it requires an extraordinarily flexible psyche to be able to complete the required volte-face at the bottom and buy the stock, market or fund after your predictions have come true, its prospects look bleak and the price has fallen.

Another way of looking at this problem is to examine how few days you need to miss being in the market to seriously damage your investment returns. If you take the decade from December 31 1994 to 2004, the S&P 500 Index produced a compound total return of 12.07 per cent each year. That's what you would have got – before costs – if you were fully invested in the index. Put another way, $10,000 invested at the outset of the 10 year period would have become $31,260 by 2004.

But what if you have tried some market timing moves and as a result missed a few days in the market, which happened to be some of its best days in that decade? What if you missed just the best 10 days? That's not much, is it – one day per year on average.

Maybe, but your return would be cut to 6.89 per cent a year and you would be left with $19,476. If you missed the best 30 days, your returns would be negative.

You may argue that you might also have missed some of the worst days, but all the evidence is that there are more good days than bad days. Do you really think you are good enough to spot those days and make sure you are fully invested and ready for them? I know I'm not.

Which brings me to my punchline: there are only two types of investors – those who know they can't make money from market timing, and those who don't know they can't. This is why I seek to follow the advice from a great investor, which is that you should buy low and sell high, but if you are buying stocks in high-quality companies, it doesn't matter if you forget the second bit. But that's an article for another day.

Part 2: sorting the wheat from the chaff

Financial Times, 15 March 2013

I ended my last article about market timing, which can be encapsulated by the mantra "buy low, sell high", by saying that if you buy shares in good companies at reasonable prices, you'll still make money even if you forget the "sell high" bit.

But what do I mean by "good companies"? If you read investment research, you will see a great deal about earnings growth, growth in earnings per share or valuations based on earnings per share. You will rarely read much about a company's return on capital employed ("ROCE").

That's a shame, because ROCE is important. If you invest your capital in a fund, a bond or a bank account, you will be very interested in the expected rate of return you will get. If you buy a share in a company, you are in effect purchasing your share of its capital. Why aren't you interested in the return it will earn on it? After all, you own part of it. Return on capital employed is usually calculated as cash operating profit divided by the sum of shareholders' equity and long-term liabilities – all numbers that can be found in a normal set of company accounts.

If, as individuals, we borrow money at a rate of say 5 per cent each year and we invest it at a return of 10 per cent a year, we will become richer. But if we earn a return of 2.5 per cent we would become poorer. The same is true of companies. Those that make a return above their cost of capital create value for their shareholders, while those that make a return below their cost of capital destroy value.

But assessing companies on this basis is less easy than just looking at earnings because of the cost of capital concept. We can easily assess the cost of a company's debt – a description of the debt profile and interest costs is usually included in the notes to a company's annual accounts – but what is the cost of its equity capital? This is the subject of much research and in reality it can only ever be an estimate. But don't let that put you off, because as an investor you should only be truly interested in companies whose returns are so high that they exceed any feasible cost of capital.

There's no need to accept my word for this. In his 1979 annual letter to Berkshire Hathaway shareholders, Warren Buffett described return on capital as the primary test of performance in managing a company. It has often puzzled me why such a clear statement from such a successful investor is so widely ignored.

You may think that your fund manager is busy using metrics such as ROCE to dig out great investments. Not in my experience. Managers will often invest in companies in industries with endemically poor returns. Why? Because they think that they can pick a point to buy the shares at which the performance of the company will improve. Maybe they expect the business cycle to pick up, or a new management team will take over, or the company itself will be taken over.

A good example of this is the airline industry, where consolidation has long been a great white hope. The International Air Transport

Association ("IATA") and the consultancy McKinsey published a report in 2011 called *Vision 2050*. It showed that there was $500bn of capital invested in the airline industry in 2010. IATA/McKinsey reckoned the industry had an overall cost of capital of 7–8 per cent a year. Comparing the returns generated with this cost of capital over the previous decade, they found that the airline industry destroyed value at the rate of about $20bn a year. During the 2002–09 business cycle, airlines' return on invested capital averaged just 2.8 per cent a year. Even in 2007 – the best year for the industry during that decade – the industry still destroyed more than $9bn of investor value on this basis. And airlines are far from alone.

The problem is that while fund managers who buy these low-return companies wait for the events which they think will change the situation, the companies destroy value. But the reverse is true when you own shares in a company that generates returns well above its cost of capital. You don't need to hold out for a takeover, a boardroom coup or a change in the business cycle, because you can be assured that its intrinsic value is growing practically every day. Time is on your side.

Part 3: never invest just to avoid tax

Financial Times, 28 March 2013

The tax year ends this coming week and if your mail is anything like mine, you are being inundated with offers of investments which qualify for tax relief provided you invest on or before April 5.

Some of these offers make sense. They are the ones in which tax relief is available for investment through a so-called "wrapper" such as an individual savings account (ISA) or a self-invested personal pension (SIPP). You don't pay any tax on capital gains realised or dividends received in your ISA, or on any funds withdrawn from it, and you can also get tax relief on contributions into SIPP. You can put sensible investments into ISAs (stocks, cash, mutual funds) and an even wider range of assets in SIPPs, including commercial property.

The problem comes when you invest mainly to obtain the tax relief, rather than because of a genuine desire to invest in the underlying assets. With enterprise investment schemes (EISs), film finance schemes and venture capital trusts (VCTs), I suspect that the main object of most investors is to avoid or defer tax rather than to access the highly restricted and specialised investments which these schemes involve.

Do you really want to invest in unquoted companies with less than £15m of gross assets, which is what is required to qualify for an EIS or a VCT? And should anyone invest in movies? Last year, Disney, which is not exactly inexperienced in the movie business, lost more than $200m on the movie *John Carter*.

We are often blinded by the ability to avoid tax. Not only does this lead us to invest in assets which we would not normally consider, but it means we tend not to look as closely at the fees which are charged. From a selection of EISs and VCTs, I found initial fees which ranged from 2 per cent to 7.5 per cent of the amount invested, charges of 2 to 3 per cent each year and performance fees, typically at 20 per cent on any gains, albeit over a hurdle rate. A product with such a rich fee structure generates a lot of sales effort, as you may also have spotted from your mailbox.

This combination of tiny, illiquid companies and high fees produces an inevitable result. Out of 131 VCTs, only 17 have a net asset value higher than the subscription price. Worse than that, the only way you can realise your investment in a VCT is to sell the shares. That is usually done not at net asset value (NAV) but at the share price which typically trails the NAV by some margin. Only five of the 131 had a share price above their issue price, partly because purchases in the secondary market don't attract tax relief.

To be fair, a lot of VCTs distribute dividends, as they are also exempt from tax, but if I look at the only VCT which I have ever invested in, the cumulative total of dividends plus NAV barely gets me back above the price at which I subscribed for the shares seven years ago. A prospectus inviting new subscriptions this tax season shows the total return since subscription excluding subscription costs as 8 per cent. That's not 8 per cent per year; it's 8 per cent in total.

You might object that I was unlucky or chose badly. But the VCT in question features in the middle of the 131 VCTs in NAV terms, and scored 86 out of a possible 100 in "Tax Efficient Review" in February.

Managers of tax-based investments seem to want investors to focus on returns after tax relief. So if you got 30 per cent income tax relief on your VCT subscription, they will try to get you to focus on the return from the 70p each £1 invested cost you after tax relief (even though the tax relief is actually applied to your tax code through self-assessment, not added to your investment as basic-rate pension tax relief is).

The flaw in this argument is that the 30p was supplied by the taxman, not by the manager, who had 100p to invest, before the not-inconsiderable fees, of course.

Rather than investing in assets you would not normally want to own through these complex, illiquid and expensive vehicles, purely to avoid tax, it is usually better to invest in things you really want to own and pay the tax due on any profits you make.

Part 4: too many stocks spoil the portfolio

Financial Times, **12 April 2013**

Portfolio diversification is a good thing. Right? Whether you reach that conclusion intuitively from the simple adage "don't put all your eggs in one basket" or have heard of modern portfolio theory, you know it makes sense.

The concept of modern portfolio theory is that a collection of investment assets has lower risk than any individual asset. This is possible because different types of assets often change in value in opposite or different ways.

But like many concepts in finance, portfolio diversification requires more than superficial examination if you are not going to get some unintended or downright poor results from applying it.

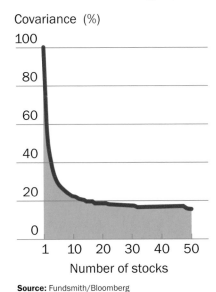

Covariance (%)

Number of stocks

Source: Fundsmith/Bloomberg

Covariance is a measure of the degree to which returns on assets move in tandem. A positive covariance means that returns move together. A negative covariance means returns move inversely. The lower the covariance number, the less risk.

Unsurprisingly, the covariance of a portfolio of FTSE 100 stocks falls as the number of stocks in the portfolio increases, but the covariance – or risk – does not fall in a straight line. The risk falls sharply as the portfolio increases in number from just one stock, but by the time it has reached about 20 to 30 stocks most of the reduction in risk that can be attained has already been achieved.

The problem is that increasing the number of stocks beyond this not only fails to achieve any significant further risk reduction, but it also leads to other problems. In "Sorting the wheat from the chaff" on March 15, I wrote about why it is important to invest in good companies. But there is a severe limit to the number of good companies available and the more stocks you own, the more you are likely to have to compromise on quality.

It is also a fact that the more stocks you own, the less you know about each of them and I have never found a theory of investment that suggests that the less you know about something, the more likely you are to generate superior returns.

There is even a term for this: "diworsification", which was coined by the legendary fund manager Peter Lynch in his book *One Up On Wall Street*. He suggested that a business that diversifies too widely risks destroying itself, because management time, energy and resources are diverted from the original investment. Similarly, adding more investments to a portfolio can lead to diworsification.

Ultimately, if you own too many stocks, your performance will match that of the benchmark or index which is composed of those stocks. There is no point in managing a portfolio or paying a fund manager to do so if you are going to do this. It is cheaper to simply buy an index fund.

Given this limitation to the benefits of diversification, why do so many fund managers own far more stocks than are necessary to obtain optimal diversification? A study from the US in 2008 *(Security Concentration and Active Fund Management: Do Focused Funds Offer Superior Performance?* by Travis Sapp and Xuemin Yan) showed that the average mutual fund manager owned a portfolio of 90 stocks, and the 20 per cent of fund managers with the most diversified portfolios owned an average of 228 stocks.

The answer is that most fund managers perceive the biggest threat to their job is not whether they lose investors' money but whether they differ from their peers. If they own so many stocks that they hug the index, they feel that they cannot be criticised.

The problem is that this behaviour, when combined with high fees for so-called active management plus overtrading, leads to an inevitable outcome: the fund underperforms the index. But this is the subject for another article.

Part 5: keep a lid on costs to protect your investment

Financial Times, **29 April 2013**

This is the final part of my series on the fundamentals of investment. So far, I have looked at why most or all of us should not try so-called market timing, and should instead focus on buying shares in good companies and holding them. I've suggested that you should never invest primarily to avoid tax, and that over-diversification in a portfolio is not only pointless but injurious to your investment performance. My last piece of advice concerns investment costs.

Even if you run a concentrated portfolio of quality shares, your returns will be constrained if you fail to control costs. Many investors are unaware of precisely how much they are being charged for their investment activity, so let's have a look at the costs the average investor might incur.

Financial advisers and wealth managers typically charge fees of 0.5–1.0 per cent on the value of the portfolio, and will often use an investment platform to hold the individual funds or shares. That might cost another 0.25 per cent a year, usually collected as "trail commission" from the underlying fund managers. The investor may also use the platform direct.

If the investments are held in mutual funds, there will be an annual management charge (AMC) of 0.75–1.5 per cent. In addition, the funds charge certain expenses to the fund: typically things such as custody, administration and legal expenses, but they have been known to charge marketing expenses too. Add that lot up and you get to what used to be called the total expense ratio and is now known as the ongoing charges figure. That's typically 1.0–1.75

per cent; add in platform and advice costs and the running total is generally between 1.75 per cent and 3 per cent.

Even that isn't it. There is also a hidden cost which is not disclosed in any of these figures: the cost of dealing within the fund. When a fund manager or an investor deals in stocks, he or she pays commissions, stamp duty at 0.5 per cent, the levy that funds the Takeover Panel and the difference between the broker's bid and offer prices (the spread). A big order in a low-liquidity share might force the price up quite a lot.

Why costs matter to investors

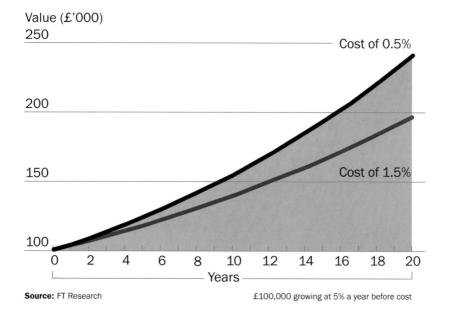

Value (£'000)

Cost of 0.5%

Cost of 1.5%

Years

Source: FT Research   £100,000 growing at 5% a year before cost

Data published in a Financial Services Authority study ("The Price of Retail Investing in the UK", by Kevin James, available at www.fsa.gov.uk) suggested that the average UK fund manager turned over about four-fifths of the portfolio each year. Apart from the questions this raises about the lack of conviction and hyperactivity, it would suggest that additional undisclosed costs of up to 1.4 per cent are being incurred each year on top of the "total" expense ratio.

All that would be bad enough, but these costs are in stark contrast to the income available from bonds and equities. The yield on the FTSE 100 is 3.8 per cent, on the S&P 500 it is 2.1 per cent and 10-year government bonds in countries such as the UK and the US yield significantly under 2 per cent. In other words, more than 100 per cent of the expected income on portfolios is being absorbed by charges.

Given this myriad of charges, you might ask how the funds are able to pay dividends. The problem is not immediately apparent, because many funds, and almost all income funds in particular, apply these charges to the capital value of the fund and not as a deduction from income. But this does not alter the fact.

John Bogle, the legendary US investor and founder of Vanguard, calculated that during the 81 years to 2007, reinvested dividend income accounted for approximately 95 per cent of the compound long-term return earned by the companies in the S&P 500. The bull markets of 1981–2000 and 2003–2007 may have misled investors into thinking that equity investment is mainly about share price appreciation. But history suggests otherwise. No one can afford to throw away all or more than all of the income from their portfolio on charges. If you do, the inevitable result is that you will experience poor performance net of these fees.

So how do you avoid or reduce charges? The obvious routes are to cut out as many of the layers of intermediation as you can between you and the actual stocks which you own. It is those layers which add to the costs. Where you can, invest direct. The other method – though it might seem odd for an active manager to advocate this – is to buy an index fund, which just tracks an index. You should be able to buy an index fund for all-in charges of 0.25 per cent a year or less.

Given that the average active fund manager underperforms the benchmark index anyway, why would you pay more?

If they use these words, don't buy their shares

The Telegraph, 18 October 2013

Having been involved in financial analysis for nearly four decades, I have increasingly formed the view that there are some words and phrases used by company managements, analysts and commentators which investors should be wary of. Apart from being an abuse of the English language, they represent a combination of woolly thinking and a desire to disguise or divert attention from a problem.

Take Wal-Mart, the US-based retailer. In a recent results presentation, the management used the term "leverage" no less than 80 times. Leverage has a legitimate meaning. It can mean to use a rigid bar to move an object. It can also mean the use of borrowing for finance which magnifies or "leverages" the operating results of a business.

It should not be used, as Wal-Mart did, to say, "Asda is a leader in online grocery delivery, and we've leveraged that experience in the US." Copied, benefited or learnt from, but not leveraged.

It is probably no coincidence that this mass outbreak of Banned Word Syndrome (or BWS, as you must have a three-letter acronym) accompanied a set of results in which Wal-Mart revealed falling sales.

So this first category of words which shouldn't be used, and which should raise your suspicions when they are, is words which are used for a meaning beyond their original purpose. Other examples include "runway" used to describe the scope for development of a product or service as in "there's plenty of runway to develop sales for this product". A runway is a strip on which an aircraft lands or takes off. You should only describe something as "key" if it relates to a lock, so no "key objectives". "Footprint" should only be used in relation to feet or footwear, not the area of operations of a business.

Another category is words which are used in an effort to sound profound, when a much simpler word exists. You will often hear management and investment analysts talking about granular data or granularity. Detail is a perfectly good word.

Sometimes the word used is not intended to convey an impression of profundity but has a pejorative or critical tone. I have lost count of the number of failed bankers and CEOs whose pension "pot" has been the subject of critical reporting and subsequent rage. I wonder if they would have suffered the same fate if it was correctly described as a pension fund. A pot is a type of container.

There are also some expressions that you should be wary of. If someone tells you they are "reaching out" to you, you might ask how this is different to or better than contacting you. And, of course, be wary of anyone who begins a statement with "to be honest", as it begs the question of whether they are normally dishonest. Always be wary of any organisation which is run by a "steering committee". Would you ever steer a boat or a car by committee, and what do you think the outcome would be if you did? Organisations run by steering committees are unlikely to achieve any good results in my view.

Which brings me on to a type of expression for which I am laying claim to a new law – Smith's Law: you should never use an expression if its opposite is so nonsensical that you would never say it. I have seen innumerable companies say they have a strategy of "select acquisitions". Would anyone ever admit to a policy of indiscriminate acquisitions (although it seems that's what many of them actually do)? The new Governor of the Bank of England, Mark Carney, has been struggling to get the markets to accept his "forward guidance" on interest rates. He might like to pause to think whether he would ever use backward guidance. If so, perhaps he would also be happy to "group together" (can you group apart?) and do some "forward planning" (what other sort is there?). Perhaps he would have more success if he just called it a prediction.

Be wary of management or commentators who engage in hyperbole. "Global" is a common example of hyperbole. Very few businesses are truly global. They may be international, but that is not the same. And when "global" is used in job titles, it is almost always an example of status inflation. Whenever I am given the business card of a head of global sales, I am tempted to ask how many globes he or she has sold. A newspaper this year ran a cycling event which it described in its advertising as "iconic". The Tour de France is iconic, but a ride around the Surrey Hills isn't.

At Fundsmith we keep a banned word count for the companies we analyse because we think they provide an insight into their management. Our investment approach is about investing in good companies. They are best spotted by their good results – we do not need managements to tell us how good they are – but when we do listen to management, the straight talkers get our vote and our money.

A classic example is Domino's Pizza, which began a turnaround in 2009 by publishing harsh criticism from its customers such as "Pizza was cardboard". You only do that if you intend to change. Since then, shares have risen from $8.50 to $68. It has been one of our largest holdings since the inception of the fund.

Chapter 4

2013–2014

3 YEARS OF...

Fundsmith Equity Fund Performance Since Inception

61.2%
Fundsmith Equity Fund

29.5%
Average IMA Global Equity Fund

1st Nov 2010 to 31st Oct 2013

NO PERFORMANCE FEES
NO INITIAL FEES
NO REDEMPTION FEES
NO OVERTRADING
NO LEVERAGE
NO SHORTING
NO HEDGING
NO DERIVATIVES
NO OVER DIVERSIFICATION
NO CLOSET INDEXING
NO LACK OF CONVICTION

Just one equity fund strategy with a small number of high quality, resilient, global growth companies that are good value and which we intend to hold for the long term, and in which we invest our own money.

An English language prospectus, a Key Investor Information Document (KIID) and a Supplementary Information Document (SID) for the Fundsmith Equity Fund are available on request and via the Fundsmith website and investors should consult these documents before purchasing shares in the fund. This financial promotion is intended for UK residents only and is communicated by Fundsmith LLP which is authorised and regulated by the Financial Conduct Authority.

Past performance is not necessarily a guide to future performance. The value of investments and the income from them may fall as well as rise and be affected by changes in exchange rates, and you may not get back the amount of your original investment. Fundsmith LLP does not offer investment advice or make any recommendations regarding the suitability of its product.

% Total Return 1st Nov - 31st Oct	2010 - 2011	2011 - 2012	2012 - 2013
Fundsmith Equity Fund[1]	+12.1	+13.7	+26.4
Average IMA Global Equity Fund[2]	+0.0	+4.3	+24.2

What Investment
Product of the Month - December 2010
Fundsmith Equity Fund

Top 100 Funds 2013
Fundsmith

Bronze

S&P CAPITAL IQ
Gold
FUND GRADING

citywire AA

www.fundsmith.co.uk
0330 123 1815

Fundsmith

[1]Source: Bloomberg T Class Accumulation Shares in GBP, net of fees, priced at midday UK time. [2]Source: Trustnet, IMA Global Growth Fund Average Performance.

Fundsmith

Why it is safe to pay up for quality

The Telegraph, 22 November 2013

Warren Buffett, the legendary investor, has described compound interest as the eighth wonder of the world. Understanding its effects is essential to success in investment. Yet it remains a mystery for many people.

The simplest illustration of this is to ask how long it takes to double your capital at 10pc a year compound return.

The whole point is that we are talking about compound returns in which the gains are added to the capital sum to which each successive period's rate of return is applied. Consequently, the answer is seven years. It only takes a compound return of 7pc per annum to double your money in 10 years.

How about this example: starting with £1,000, what is the difference in final capital from 30 years of investment at 10pc a year compound versus 30 years at 12.5pc a year? I ask this because it may represent a reasonable range of outcomes from an investment lifetime in which a person saves for 30 years before retiring then trying to live on the income from investments. The answer, rather surprisingly, is that the extra 2.5pc of compound return would double the final sum – so £1,000 invested would become £34,243 at 12.5pc as opposed to £17,449 at 10pc.

At Fundsmith, we only invest in companies which make high returns on capital employed; convert most or all of their profits into cash; have high profit margins; and which have proved resilient to economic cycles over many decades.

But the valuation of such companies has become a subject of concern to investors. Their valuations have risen through the financial crisis and the "Great Recession" which has followed. This is because they produce consistent performance from the provision of our everyday necessities and luxuries, and have an ability to grow in a world in which there has been little or no economic growth in contrast to most other sectors of the market.

Since the rise in their share prices has outpaced the rise in the companies' profits or cash flows in recent years, they are certainly more highly rated than they were, but that is not the same as being overvalued. While I accept that they are not as attractively valued as they were before this recent rise, I would suggest a study of compounding should perhaps give reason to pause before moving swiftly on to the presumption that as a result they should be sold or even avoided.

We don't often look at price to earnings (p/e) ratios, the traditional measure of value, at Fundsmith as we prefer to look at cash flows, but since almost everybody else uses them, it is the simplest way of expressing the relative valuation of our portfolio, which currently has a p/e about two points higher than the market – the Fundsmith stocks are on about 21 times forecast earnings and the MSCI World Index is on about 19 times.

In judging what this implies, there are a number of things which you should also be aware of, namely that not all earnings (the "e" in that ratio) are of equal value. The shares in the Fundsmith portfolio produce their earnings with significantly less capital intensity (hence their higher return on capital) than the market in general, and they deliver more of their earnings in cash, which is more valuable. Their earnings are also more predictable, which brings me back to compounding.

I have taken a look at how much you could have paid for some of these companies over the 30-year period between 1979 and 2009. In particular, I looked at Coca-Cola and Colgate-Palmolive. In 1979 they had about the same rating as the market – 10 times earnings. But what could you have paid for them at that time in terms of p/e and still equalled the performance of the market over the next 30 years? The answer rather surprisingly is about 40 times earnings. Why? Because these companies' total returns grew at about 5pc a year faster than the market over this period, and rather like the earlier illustration of a 2.5pc differential in compound growth, this 5pc differential multiplied the final capital sum represented by their share prices four times faster than the market rose.

Of course, the next 30 years may be different. However, if I had to guess how it would affect this calculation, it would be that companies like Coke and Colgate will fare even better in terms of growth given that cyclical stocks are unlikely to get a repetition of the growth that was stimulated by the credit bubble. It is also fair to point out that quality stocks may indeed not be expensive relative to the rest of the market but that both will prove to be expensive, particularly when interest rates rise. But even so, I suggest you consider how you might have reacted if someone had suggested you invest in Coca-Cola or Colgate at, say, twice the market p/e in 1979. In rejecting that idea, you would have missed the chance to make twice as much money as an investment in the market indices over that period.

It's déjà vu all over again

Financial Times, 6 December 2013

Peter "Yogi" Berra was a baseball player for the New York Yankees, and managed both the Yankees and their New York rivals, the Mets. He's also famous for a series of deceptively simple witticisms known as Yogi-isms which are often contradictory – as in "Nobody goes there any more. It's too crowded." One of my favourites – "It's déjà vu all over again" – might have been invented for the investment industry.

Time and again we are told that someone has devised a new technique of investing, or a new investment product. The truth is that in this area of human endeavour there are few, if any, new products or methods. By and large, we have seen it all before.

For example, we mostly think that pensions are a 20th century phenomenon. The first state pension was implemented in the UK in 1909, and occupational pension schemes providing benefits for company employees had their heyday after the Second World War.

Once you reach retirement, you are generally required to use your pension fund to purchase an annuity from an insurer which provides the pension income. Or at least, that's the theory. Latterly, one of the problems encountered by pension funds has been the general improvement in longevity. Pensioners are living longer, which has increased the liabilities of pension funds and so strained their funding.

Our 17th century forebears would have known all about that. They encountered these same problems over 300 years ago and developed products called tontines to deal with them. A tontine is an investment plan named after a banker, Lorenzo de Tonti, who is credited with inventing it in France in 1653. Each subscriber paid a sum into the tontine, and thereafter received an annuity. Sound familiar? As members died, their shares transferred to the other participants, and so the value of each remaining annuity increased. On the death of the last member, the scheme was wound up.

Tontines were relatively widespread in the 18th and 19th centuries. France established a state tontine in 1689. The English government organised one in 1693. But tontines soon caused problems. Their structure created an obvious incentive for members to kill each other, one reason why they are often used as a plot device in murder mysteries. And just as they have today, governments running tontines tended to underestimate the longevity of the population.

What's the purpose of this history lesson? It is that you might be well advised to check the history of any investment product you are offered to see how it has fared in the past, even if it was called something else at the time.

Take so-called precipice bonds. Typically, this is an investment product offering an eye-catchingly high yield – 10 per cent is not that unusual. Of course, it's easy to sell investors something they are desperate for – such as high yield in a low-yield environment – and salesmen use this craving to encourage investors to overlook the pitfalls. The catch with a precipice bond is that the investor may not get all of his or her capital back. The yield is typically supplied by collecting premiums for writing put options (which oblige the option writer to buy at a fixed price) based on a given scenario, such as a fall in the stock market over the period of the bond.

Why the term precipice? High option premiums can be obtained for writing put options on something very volatile which is trading at a record high. Precipice bonds first came to my attention in 1999 at the peak of the dotcom boom, when several such bonds were floated with high yields obtained by writing put options on tech stocks, which were then at record highs.

Investors subsequently lost much of their capital when the options were exercised. The option writers – their bond funds – were obliged to buy the tech stocks at the peak prices at which the options had been struck, even though market prices were by now well below those levels. The investors were metaphorically looking over the edge of a precipice in financial terms at the moment they accepted the risk that tech stocks might fall.

Needless to say, "precipice bonds" is a colloquial term. They were marketed with much more mundane names, such as stock market income bonds, so as not to scare investors or give too many clues to their true risks.

But surely people have learnt that lesson? I'm not sure they have. In January, Goldman Sachs sold "Autocallable Contingent Coupon Buffered Equity-Linked Medium-Term Notes" (here's a clue: what does it do? If you don't understand it, don't invest) yielding 10 per cent plus some upside tied to the performance of Apple's common stock. But if Apple shares dropped, the notes would decline at the same rate. Apple shares were over $500 at the time the instrument was created. They have been below $400 this year. The notes were sold the day before the company announced a set of earnings that sent its share price down 12 per cent. Investors bought a total of $1.75bn of structured notes linked to Apple in 2012.

As the old adage goes: "There are no new jokes, only some people who haven't heard them before."

Fundsmith

Just the facts when weighing investments

Financial Times, **24 January 2014**

In the 1950s, an early detective series on TV was *Dragnet*, starring the fictional Joe Friday. In the opening sequence to every show he would say: "My name is Friday. I'm a cop." His other famous one-liner, usually delivered while trying to extract evidence from a hapless babbling witness, was: "Just the facts."

We would all do well to remember Joe's witness interview technique when it comes to investing. So let's start with a few facts – those shown in the table below. Would you want to own a company which had delivered those results?

Year	Revenue	Operating cash flow
2006	44.3	14.4
2007	51.1	17.8
2008	60.4	21.6
2009	58.5	19.0
2010	62.5	21.1
2011	70.0	27.0
2012	73.7	31.6

It has seen revenues rise by 66 per cent over the past six years, a compound growth rate of 8.8 per cent, which was no mean feat for a period which spanned the financial crisis and a deep recession. The company experienced a downturn in 2009, but revenues only fell by 3 per cent, so it is barely cyclical.

Its cash flow performance has been even better. Operating cash flows grew by 119 per cent over the same period – a compound annual growth rate of 14 per cent – and its operating cash flows are 43 per cent of its revenues, so its margins are exceptionally good.

All in all, it's an impressive operating performance. Of course, you can't make an investment decision on the basis of that alone.

You'd need some data on valuation – and you could be forgiven for thinking that, given its recent record, its shares must be so highly valued as to be uninvestable.

What if I told you that you could currently buy this company on a free cash flow yield (the free cash flow it generates, divided by its market value) of over 8 per cent? That it is on a prospective price/earnings ratio of 12? It pays dividends too – giving a 3.2 per cent yield covered 2.4 times. To cap it all, it has cash on its balance sheet equivalent to about a quarter of its market value.

"How do I buy the shares?" might well be your response. It was certainly mine. If you put a dollar sign at the beginning of those figures and "billions" after them, the company I have described is Microsoft.

At this point, I would guess that investors who might have been salivating at the prospect of this investment opportunity will be surprised. Surely Microsoft is a loser in the tech wars? I have lost count of the number of articles I have read in computer publications, business magazines, newspapers, analysts' reports and blogs questioning whether Microsoft can "save itself".

Save itself from what? Bears argue that Microsoft has lost out to Apple in mobile devices and Google in online search and mobile operating systems. It is also inextricably linked to the declining PC replacement cycle as that uses its Windows operating system, which is the Microsoft product most of us know.

That is certainly the view you will get if you read most commentary on Microsoft. However, back to those pesky facts. Microsoft's largest division by both revenues and profits is its servers and tools division which develops and markets software for servers and software developer tools. Its customers are IT professionals and software developers. How much do you know about that?

If you use Microsoft software in work, and the vast majority of us do, then I would guess that you have gone through, or are about to go through, an upgrade from Windows XP to Windows 7 as Microsoft is halting support for the older product. Windows XP runs 95 per cent of the world's cash machines. This is an example of a gift which keeps on giving – an annuity income for Microsoft which results from us all having to update to more recent versions of its operating system.

I do not profess to know anything about technology investment (although at least with this awareness of my limitations, I suspect I am one step ahead of most of those who think they do). Nor do I have any insight into who will take over from Steve Ballmer as chief executive. But I do know something about financial analysis, which often seems to be ignored, as it has been by many commentators on Microsoft.

Worse, much of the "research" and commentary about Microsoft is not about whether it is doing well or badly. It's more about the biases of the commentators, who often seem to feel that because Microsoft is not hip or fashionable, and doesn't have the design sense of Apple, it doesn't deserve to succeed.

The facts suggest otherwise. Just stick to the facts.

Shale: miracle, revolution or bandwagon?

Financial Times, **7 February 2014**

Unless you have been in hibernation for the past few years, you will have heard that there is a shale hydrocarbon "revolution" or "miracle" under way. Barack Obama, the US president, pledged support for shale gas development in his 2012 State of the Union speech. David Cameron has urged opponents of fracking to "get on board".

"Fracking" has passed into the vernacular. The term was added to the Oxford English Dictionary last June. It involves releasing a high-pressure mix of water, sand and chemicals to crack rocks and release oil and gas from shale. Environmentalists have all sorts of objections to this practice. And there are other problems with the concept of shale as a saviour – either in terms of cheap energy or as an investment.

The first is the concept of "energy return on energy investment" or EROEI. This is the ratio of the amount of energy generated from an energy source to the amount of energy expended to obtain that energy. It is an important and mostly ignored ratio which determines both the efficiency of our economies – how much of our resources have to be expended into getting our energy – and the economics of energy exploration and generation.

The oil discoveries which took place a century or more ago were mostly in onshore locations, often in politically stable countries and close to key consumer markets.

However, there is a natural tendency to pick the low hanging fruit first, and over time, oil and gas exploration and production has, out of necessity, moved to less hospitable and remote locations, which

US oil and gas
EROEI estimations

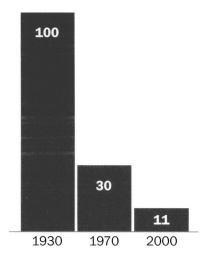

Source: www.theoildrum.com

place logistical barriers between oil and gas and the markets.

Shale gas/oil and fracking are just an extension of this trend. US oil production had an EROEI of 100:1 in the 1930s – every hundred units produced required one unit to be expended. By 2000, despite huge technological advances, that had dropped to 11:1. The ratio for shale oil is about 5:1. This is a critical difference.

There is also the issue of depletion. An old trick in investment analysis is to ask whether an annual return of £20 for an investment of £100 is good or bad. Most people will say it is a good return. But you lack other vital information necessary to assess the investment: the asset life and maturity value. If the asset only lasts for three years and is then worthless, it is a bad investment, as you will only recoup £60 in total from £100 invested. If it lasts for 20 years, it's a good investment, as you will recoup £400.

Asset life is critical to assess all investments. In the case of oil and gas exploration and production, it is the period until the well or field is no longer economically viable and has to be abandoned.

The steepness of decline in production rates for shale oil wells has been a surprise. A typical well in the Bakken Formation, North Dakota, drilled in 2012 is likely to be producing at less than 30 per cent of its initial production rate today. Recent disappointing performance relative to expectations at the newer Utica shale play in the northeast US and Canada mirrors this.

Investor returns on shale gas investments have broadly come in two main periods. From the discovery of most shale gas in 2002 until 2007, share prices of shale companies rose rapidly. Once the newly discovered gas came on stream, natural gas prices fell – and so did returns and share prices. The largest shale player in the UK is Cuadrilla Resources, which was founded in 2007 and is owned by AJ Lucas, Riverstone Holdings and Carlyle and is exploring for shale gas deposits in Lancashire. AJ Lucas, a quoted Australian company, owns 42 per cent of Cuadrilla. Its own shares are just a quarter of what they were worth in 2009.

Nor is this disappointing performance limited to small companies. BP wrote off $1bn on shale in July 2012 whilst the Canadian company Encana said it lost almost $2bn on its shale gas assets in recent years. Shell is selling its stake in the Eagle Ford shale reserve in Texas, having written off more than $2bn on its assets there. It claims more than 200 wells are incapable of reaching their production target. Peter Voser, the former Shell chief executive, has said the rhetoric about the US shale revolution being exported to other countries was "hyped", and that the rest of the world was in an early "exploration phase" which could yield "negative surprises".

Fundsmith

As the late Jimmy Goldsmith was fond of saying: "If you see a bandwagon, it's too late." The shale bandwagon may already have passed.

Investors are their own worst enemies

The Telegraph, **14 February 2014**

Michael Johnson, the former American sprinter, once said: "The only one who can beat me is me." I suspect that this statement simply demonstrates a lack of modesty, but it can have another, subtler meaning: that even if we are good at what we do, we are capable of producing a bad result because we allow our own emotions to defeat us. So often we are defeated not by our competition or the difficulty of the task but by our own psyche.

In investment it is easy, and indeed accurate, to criticise the poor service which much of the fund management industry provides to investors and to identify this as a major reason why investors get such poor returns.

Most managers do not regard the biggest threat to their career as losing investors' money or performing badly. They regard the biggest threat as differing from their peers. The only thing that they regard as worse than failing is standing out from the crowd.

Never mind that they and their fellow fund managers produce dire results for investors: if they all perform roughly the same, they are unlikely to see mass withdrawals by savers or get fired from their jobs. This leads the majority of "long-only" fund managers (those who do not use the sophisticated techniques of "short selling") to buy so many shares that they more or less replicate the performance of whatever index is their performance benchmark. I say "more or less" but the reality is that they mostly produce less.

If a fund manager owns enough shares to roughly track an index – and you don't need more than about 25 randomly chosen shares to do so in most markets – their fund will underperform the index once it has suffered from the fund manager's fees and the cost of his or her dealing activity. This outcome is as inevitable as it is poor.

I have lost count of the number of investors who have told me that they have withdrawn their savings from a long-term savings plan or personal pension only to discover that the amount realised is approximately the same as the amount subscribed over many years or decades, any gains that were realised having been swallowed by fees. One investor I know claims to have gained more from compensation from mis-selling than from the investment returns on her savings.

The situation doesn't appear to be any better with hedge funds. The HSBC Investment Funds Performance Review shows that on average hedge funds have underperformed the market for five years in a row. One of my colleagues who recently applied to withdraw his investment from such a hedge fund was asked why.

He said it was due to the poor performance, to which the fund manager responded that almost all hedge funds had underperformed in recent years. Perhaps unsurprisingly, this did not provide much comfort. It's that herd instinct again. The fund managers feel that they can justify their position if they all fail together.

Collectively, fund managers ignore Sir John Templeton's axiom that "If you do what everyone else does, you will get what everyone else gets."

As a result of all this group think, the average US fund investor over the past 20 years has earned a return of 7pc a year below the market (Dalbar Statistics) because of poor performance of the fund, fees and their own poor timing.

There is not much point in trying to negotiate your way around the poor performance of the fund management industry if you are going to make matters worse by your own actions. And we are certainly capable of doing that even when the fund manager does well.

Between 2000 and 2010, the best performing US fund was the CGM Focus Fund, which delivered annualised returns of 18pc a year. Mightily impressive. Over the same period, the average investor in the fund lost 11pc a year. Investors showed an unerring ability to buy into the fund at its peak in valuation and sell out at its troughs.

The vast majority of us are terrible at so-called "market timing", in which investors try to sell at or close to market peaks and buy at market lows. All the statistics about investor flows show that believing you can accomplish this feat is the triumph of hope over experience. The wisest investors who are most likely to get the best performance are those who have at least realised that they can't do this successfully and so don't try.

The other major fault that most investors have, whether private investors or professional fund managers, is that they are too active – they deal too much.

Leaving aside the fact that if our timing decisions are almost all bad we would be better off making as few as possible, all dealing activity has a cost, much of which is hidden. We are taught that to be successful investors, we need up-to-the-minute information and the ability to deal instantaneously. In fact, nothing could be further from the truth.

We should instead emulate the favourite client of fund manager Jonathan Ruffer, who said that "he would be monitoring performance on a quarterly basis, and if, after the first 25 years…"

It is a sobering thought: the fund management industry may serve us badly as investors, but there is one thing more detrimental to our wealth than that – us.

Big Blue investors may not have a winning hand

Financial Times, 24 February 2014

In 2011, the legendary investor Warren Buffett caused a stir by announcing Berkshire Hathaway's first major investment in a technology company, an area of the market he had always avoided, claiming that he didn't understand it.

This approach accorded well with his advice that investors should always stick to investing within their so-called "circle of competence". Most sensible investors would agree with this idea; after all, who would embrace a strategy of investing in companies or assets you don't understand? In my experience, however, many investors still fail to realise how narrow their circle of competence is.

Buffett's purchase was over $10bn of stock in technology company IBM, making it Berkshire's second-largest portfolio investment after Coca-Cola and turning Berkshire into IBM's largest shareholder.

Since his purchase, IBM has reported falling revenues. The fourth quarter of 2013 was the seventh in a row in which revenues were lower than they had been in the equivalent quarter the year before. The chief executive and other senior executives have volunteered to forego their bonuses for 2013 as a result of this poor performance. As the Lex column of the FT said recently, "IBM quarterly results practically write themselves now: dreadful revenue growth accompanied by cost controls, share buybacks and dividends that combine to make the technology legend look somewhat less bad than the top line would suggest."

It so happens that I was looking at IBM at about the same time as Warren Buffett was accumulating his stake, but I decided to avoid it. Why?

A couple of features about IBM unsettled me. One was that they had announced a "road map" to generate growth in earnings per share (EPS) to $20 by 2015, up from $11.50 in 2010. I do not like management that uses terms such as "road map" unless they are discussing driving cars. "Plan" is a perfectly good word.

I also dislike the focus on EPS. Not all earnings are created equal. Some require greater or lesser amounts of capital to generate them and not all are delivered in cash. This should come as no surprise to Mr Buffett, who identified return on capital as the primary test of company performance in his 1979 annual chairman's letter. Much EPS growth is generated at the expense of return on capital and so destroys value.

But if the focus on EPS growth was worrying, the planned means of achieving this identified in the "road map" was even more troubling: roughly 40 per cent revenue growth, including acquisitions, 30 per cent operating leverage and 30 per cent share buybacks.

Revenue growth is a higher-quality source of value creation than share buybacks or cost control (which is what I take it IBM means by "operating leverage"), provided it is not achieved at the expense of returns. I am wary of revenue growth achieved through acquisitions, the majority of which do not create value. However, there is at least no limit to revenue growth, while cost-cutting and buybacks are both finite.

Moreover, although some buybacks create value for shareholders, many do not and are executed seemingly irrespective of the valuation of the shares. A company cannot create value for remaining shareholders if it pays more for the shares it buys than their intrinsic value, but many companies (and investors) are fooled by the familiar boast that buybacks are accretive to EPS. In an age where the alternative use of cash often generates little income because interest rates are close to zero, almost any alternative is accretive to EPS, but it does not necessarily create value.

I found a five-year plan for significant share buybacks particularly disturbing. How can the management possibly know whether the shares will trade sufficiently below intrinsic value to create value-enhancing buyback opportunities on such a scale and so far ahead?

One other feature of IBM struck me in 2010 when my Fundsmith colleagues and I were reading the company's 2009 annual report. We noticed that it had a $1.9bn error in its cash flow statement. We rang IBM to check that we were not misinterpreting it, and they confirmed we were correct and that we were the only people who had asked about it.

Maybe others had discovered it and didn't bother to call, but I suspect the reality is that very few investors or analysts read annual reports and 10k filings any more. The error was corrected in the 2010 annual report and did not materially affect my view of IBM, but it certainly affected my view of those who were analysing it.

What did you invest in before the war, great-grandpa?

Financial Times, **8 March 2014**

In this centenary year of what contemporaries called the Great War and we now call the First World War – because it became necessary to number them – what can we learn from the changes in the constituents of the stock market over the intervening century?

The problem in attempting to answer this question is that most of the major stock market indices on which we now rely were devised long after 1914.

Looking at the world's two most significant equity markets, London and New York, Standard & Poor's first introduced what is now the S&P 500 index in 1923, and it has only existed in its current form since 1957.

The FTSE 100 is of even more recent vintage having only come into existence in 1984. Even the much less representative FT 30 share index was devised in 1935.

The only index from either side of the Atlantic that existed when Gavrilo Princip's fateful shot echoed around the world, and which still exists today, is the Dow Jones Industrial Average, established by Charles Dow in 1884. By 1914 the Dow consisted of 10 companies. Today it contains 30.

The constituents in 1914 show that the commanding heights of the US economy were occupied by heavy industrial companies. They were manufacturers, mostly of basic materials consumed by other manufacturers.

Only one company made it into both lists: General Electric.

Even so, its business has changed radically over the century. Nearly half of its revenues now come from aero engines and financial services – two businesses that did not exist in 1914, since Wilbur and Orville Wright had only taken to the skies just over a decade earlier.

Just two of the 1914 companies, Amalgamated Copper and Central Leather, have actually ceased to exist.

The remainder have disappeared from prominence and no longer form part of any index, apart from US Steel, which has not made a profit since 2008.

Today's index is dominated by companies of a very different ilk.

Five are involved in financial services, if you include Visa, which is a payment processor.

Four are involved in computer hardware, software or services; four are in the drug or healthcare sector; and four are in consumer goods or fast food.

Two are oil companies, two are in retailing and two are telecoms companies. The aerospace industry has Boeing, but is also represented within GE and United Technologies, which makes Sikorsky helicopters and Pratt & Whitney engines. There is one entertainment company (Walt Disney). The only companies which look anything like the 1914 vintage are 3M and chemicals group Du Pont.

What should we conclude from this?

The idea of investing with a century as a time horizon is clearly unrealistic. Not much lasts forever in the world of equity investment. If you had invested a trust in the Dow constituents for the benefit of your descendants before you marched off to the western front in 1914, and locked it away for the next century, your great-grandchildren would now be mightily bemused by its contents.

If instead you had invested in the companies which rose to the top of the Dow, in terms of market capitalisation, you would certainly have done better (even though these companies may have become large partly by issuing large amounts of equity on which they have made inadequate returns).

But the position of these companies offers some clue to what is regarded as representative of the dominant sectors of the economy now and then.

In so doing it serves to remind us that the US economy, somewhat like the UK economy, is increasingly post-industrial with a growing reliance on financial services, consumers and healthcare.

Finally, the evolution of the Dow shows it is better to invest in companies that make aeroplanes (and their engines) than those that fly them – there isn't a single airline in the Dow.

Why buy Brics when you can have Mugs?

Financial Times, 11 April 2014

Perhaps the most dangerous investment concept is the "no brainer". Take emerging markets equities as an example. They should surely have much better returns than those in developed economies, as they mostly have better demographics with young, fast-growing populations; higher GDP growth; and they didn't suffer the meltdown from the collapse of their banking systems that plagued the US and Europe.

How to play this theme? Most would buy an actively managed emerging markets equity fund. If you did so in the past few years, you have almost certainly suffered disappointment.

Over the past five years, the average return for the funds in the Investment Management Association's Global Emerging Markets sector was 65.7 per cent. They underperformed the MSCI Emerging Markets Index, which rose by 69 per cent over the same period.

Nothing new here, you might well think – the average active manager underperforms the benchmark, often owning so many shares that the fund becomes a "closet index tracker", replicating the performance of the index but with the added drag of fees and dealing costs. Far from being a surprise, underperformance is a near-certainty.

You could avoid it by investing in an index fund instead. Had you bought a fund that tracked the MSCI EM Index you would indeed have fared better over the past few years.

But you would still have done significantly worse than if you had bought a fund that tracks a developed-world benchmark; the FTSE

Fundsmith

100 is up by 102 per cent and the S&P 500 by 124 per cent over the same period. Faced with this experience, it must be tempting for investors to conclude that the assumption of superior returns from emerging markets is just plain wrong.

But the peak of disappointment would be if you had bought into one of the most popular themes of emerging market investing over the past decade and put money into a Bric fund. The acronym Bric was coined by Jim O'Neill, then an economist at Goldman Sachs, in 2001 and stands for Brazil, Russia, India and China. It was supposed to identify the four economic powerhouses of the future, and plenty of passive and active products have been constructed and promoted around it.

Surely few EM investments can have performed better than a Bric fund? Wrong again. Over the past five years, the MSCI Bric Index is up just 44 per cent, underperforming both emerging markets generally and developed markets such as the US and UK. Needless to say, the average Bric active fund has also underperformed the Bric Index too.

A big reason for this disappointment lies in what makes up these indices. The largest companies, which dominate the EM Index, are Asian consumer electronics companies, Chinese banks and internet companies, phone companies and Russian energy companies. I would regard all of these companies as uninvestable. In the case of the banks in particular, their risk exposure is opaque. I wouldn't invest in a bank in the UK, so what would possess anyone to trust the accounts of a Chinese bank? Yet the largest sector by far in the EM Index representing over a quarter of it is financials.

The companies that I would regard as most investable are consumer staples. These represent just 8 per cent of the EM Index.

So it is no surprise to me that the EM Index, its tracker funds and the closet trackers among the active funds who secretly track it too have performed badly.

Investing in an index of the Brics is a leap of faith for another reason. The Heritage Foundation, a US think-tank, publishes an annual report using a factor model, which attempts to rank countries in an Index of Economic Freedom.

The index assesses how attractive they are for business and investment based on data on a series of factors including property rights, corruption, size of government, regulation, flexibility of labour and liberality of markets.

Places such as Singapore, Switzerland and Hong Kong rank near the top. The highest-ranked Bric is Brazil at number 114 (out of 186), followed by India at 120, China at 137 and Russia down in 140th position.

If you were willing to invest on the basis of a snappy acronym with no regard for the economic and political characteristics of the countries, perhaps you should have subscribed for a fund investing in a group of countries which each rank a little ahead of the Brics in terms of Economic Freedom. Forget the Mints or the Civets – how about Moldova (110), Uganda (91), Greece (119) and Suriname (130)? These I have christened the Mugs, a pretty good description of anyone who would invest on this basis.

A Hitchhiker's Guide to emerging markets

Financial Times, 1 August 2014

In my last column for *FT Money* I tried to get to the bottom of why so many investors have had such a bad experience pursuing the superior economic growth in emerging markets. This begs a further question: is there a better way to invest in the developing world?

Growth is often achieved only at the expense of returns on capital and so does not create any value for shareholders. This problem is sometimes ignored by investors hungry for growth, particularly so in emerging markets where superior growth rates are such a significant part of the rationale for investment.

When a company makes an inadequate return on capital – which I will define as one below its cost of capital – it destroys value. Far from growing and employing more of their capital, shareholders should want such a business to shrink its operations and return any cash liberated as a result.

So where can you find companies with consistently high returns on capital and which are capable of profitable growth?

One of the clearest trends after the Second World War has been the rise of the middle class or consumers. In emerging markets there are various definitions of what constitutes this class, but one of the commonly accepted cut-off points is around $10 per day in disposable income. Below this level, individuals cannot afford to be consumers. Their life is one of subsistence.

Out of a world population of 2.5bn in 1950, probably only some 300m were consumers by this definition. By 2010 this had become 2.4bn out of a total population of 6.8bn. Extrapolation is a dangerous forecasting technique but by 2025 it is estimated (by Groningen University, the Brookings Institute and McKinsey) that out of an estimated world population of 7.9bn, 4.2bn will be consumers.

More importantly, it is expected that the growth rate in consumption in emerging markets will be more than three times that in the developed world.

The ranks of the middle-class consumer are expected to be swelled by >1bn between 2010 and 2020. On the chart shown, it is sobering to note that the UK, and indeed the whole of Europe, is included in the small box in the top right-hand corner labelled "all other".

The Hitchhiker's Guide to the Galaxy discovers that the entry for Earth in the Guide consists in its entirety of the word "harmless". His friend Ford Prefect, a contributor to the Guide, tells him that the next edition will contain an updated entry on Earth that Ford has been researching. It will read: "mostly harmless".

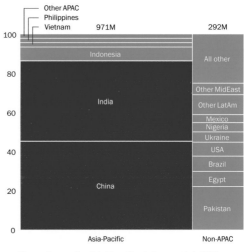

Distribution of growth of middle class 2010–2020

Source: Euromonitor; Bain Macro Trends Group analysis, 2011

What Arthur Dent is forced to come to terms with is that his home planet is not particularly significant in cosmic terms. Similarly, as investors, we would do well to realise that our home market, the one with which we are most familiar, is not that important.

This is certainly so in terms of growth in consumer spending. A strategy that relied solely on such growth in the developed world would at best be forgoing better opportunities elsewhere – which is exactly why so many multinationals in consumer sectors are focused on growing their business in emerging markets.

Ally this to the consistent high returns on capital that many consumer companies are able to sustain and you have an investment strategy with the potential for superior returns. Consumer staples companies generate those returns as their combination of brands, pricing power, distribution and control of their supply chain helps fend off competition.

A strategy of investing in consumer staples companies with the bulk of their operations in developing markets has substantially outperformed the other emerging markets investment strategies that I reviewed in my previous article, over the past five to 10 years. Of course, the past is an imperfect guide to the future but it would be unwise to ignore the rapid and predictable growth in consumption of everyday necessities and luxuries when considering investment in emerging markets.

How investors ignored the warning signs at Tesco

Financial Times, 6 September 2014

Since starting Fundsmith, the stock which I have most frequently been asked about, and implored to buy, is Tesco. Yes, the same Tesco which has just issued two profit warnings within six weeks, which has cut its interim dividend by 75 per cent and has a share price which has fallen to its 2003 level.

I was even asked about it at one of the fund's annual meetings, and a member of the audience tweeted afterwards of his incredulity that I had not been pressed further on the subject.

Superficially it's easy to see why. We are talking not just about the UK's most powerful retailer which has underperformed the market for several years, thereby attracting investors who rely on the theory that what goes down must come up (ignoring the fact that Sir Isaac Newton popularised a theory which proclaims the opposite) and so might present a buying opportunity.

Tesco: the Leahy years

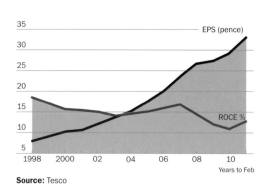

Source: Tesco

Furthermore, this is a UK stock owned by Warren Buffett, the "Sage of Omaha". In the face of such endorsement, how could I resist owning this gem?

There are many reasons why I am unlikely ever to own a retailer in the Fundsmith Equity Fund, but when it comes to Tesco, a single lesson from the Sage himself was enough to put me off.

In his 1979 letter to shareholders, Mr Buffett stated: "The primary test of managerial economic performance is the achievement of a high earnings rate on equity capital employed (without undue leverage, accounting gimmickry, etc.) and not the achievement of consistent gains in earnings per share."

This makes it all the more surprising to me that both Mr Buffett and the many acolytes who have seemingly followed him to the gates of hell in Tesco, ignored this chart.

This is not the first such chart that I have come across in which a company reports steadily rising earnings per share (EPS), on which most analysts and "investors" focus.

For them, the rise in EPS seems to have a mesmeric effect like Kaa, the snake in *The Jungle Book*. But they ignore the point that more capital is being employed to generate those earnings at ever lower returns. Add in the fact that Tesco has changed its definition of return on capital employed (ROCE) eight times during those years, and there's more than enough material to send investors running for cover – even those who have less aversion than I do to retailers.

Yet much of the commentary about what has gone wrong at Tesco focuses on Philip Clarke, who took over as chief executive from Sir Terry Leahy in 2011, as if everything was going swimmingly until then. Looking at the ROCE line in the chart, it is clear that this was not the case.

Moreover, one thing to bear in mind is that if Tesco's ROCE during the Leahy years fell from a very good 19 per cent to a less than adequate 10 per cent, this is an average of returns on capital employed, which includes both capital invested years ago and more recent commitments.

To drag the average ROCE down so dramatically, it is likely that returns on new investments in those years were not just inadequate, but in some cases negative – as the ill-starred US expansion proved to be.

Even if return on capital employed does not have the same importance for you as it does for me, or the Sage (at least in 1979), consider this: in 14 of the past 18 years (taking us back to 1997 when Sir Terry became chief executive), Tesco's free cash flow less its dividend (with free cash defined as operating cash flow less gross capital expenditure) was a negative number.

In plain English, Tesco was not generating enough cash both to invest and to pay its dividend. In half of those 14 years, the proceeds of fixed asset disposals took the numbers back into the black, but that is not exactly a sustainable source of financing.

So guess what they did instead? Yes, they borrowed it. Tesco's gross debt, which was £894m when Sir Terry took over, peaked at nearly £15.9bn in 2009. The company spent much of its free cash on fixed asset investment and raised debt to help pay the dividend. This is neither healthy nor sustainable, as investors in Tesco have now come to realise.

The concept that this might not be sustainable hardly requires much thought. Neither does charting the ROCE versus the growth in EPS. Yet it is evident that many investors, including it seems the Sage of Omaha (who has been trimming his Tesco stake in recent years) either didn't do this or ignored the results if they did. It makes me wonder what else they are ignoring.

Eureka! I discovered how funds are named

Financial Times, **3 October 2014**

**Last month Calpers, the California Public Employees'
Retirement Scheme, one of the world's largest pension
funds, announced it was withdrawing its $4bn investment in
hedge funds. This raises some serious issues, not the least
of which is why it invested in hedge funds in the first place.**

In its fiscal year ended June 30 2014, Calpers earned just 7.1 per
cent on its hedge fund portfolio compared with 18.4 per cent on
its fund overall. But 2013–2014 was not a uniquely bad year for
hedge funds and neither was Calpers' poor experience unusual.
The average hedge fund returned an average of 7.4 per cent in
2013, underperforming the S&P 500 Index by 23 per cent and
underperforming the market for the fifth straight year.

In a sense, the underperformance of hedge funds against a
benchmark is not the main problem for a fund such as Calpers
which should probably ignore index benchmarks anyway, but the
underperformance of hedge funds compared to what Calpers can
and has achieved in other investments is more problematic – as is
the fact that it paid $135m in fees in 2013–2014 to those hedge
funds.

In his 2012 book *The Hedge Fund Mirage*, Simon Lack presented
evidence that over the period 1998–2010, hedge fund managers'
fees accounted for between 86 per cent and 98 per cent of total
returns earned. The term "hedge fund" has become a means of
describing a fee structure which benefits the fund managers rather
than a description of any particular methodology of investment.

The defence which is sometimes raised for hedge funds is that this underperformance is not a good reason to abandon them, as their strategies are uncorrelated to the general trend in markets and that will prove worthwhile when markets go into reverse. This would be more credible if it weren't for their lamentable performance during the financial crisis of 2008–2009 when so many of them proved to be leveraged long-only funds rather than hedged in any way which would justify the name.

However, there may have been another way of spotting the incipient problem in Calpers' hedge fund portfolio. Of the 24 hedge funds involved, no less than 11 had the word Eureka in their title. "Eureka!" is the translation of an ancient Greek word meaning "I have found it!" which Archimedes is alleged to have exclaimed upon discovering the way to measure the volume of an irregular object by measuring its displacement of water. More recently, it became a term associated with the discovery of gold, especially in the California gold rush of the 1840–1850s.

Naming your fund after such a well-known scientific discovery or finding riches was setting yourself up for a fall or your investors for disappointment, but it was clearly of great benefit if you were trying to market your fund to Calpers.

This brings me to the subject of fund names. You may be familiar with the concept of the circle of competence, often quoted by the great investor Warren Buffett and his partner Charlie Munger. The idea is that you are only likely to succeed in investing if you stick to investing in things which you understand, which seems intuitively obvious but is often disregarded by many investors.

Names of funds are often a clue to the fact that you may not understand what they do (or perhaps aren't meant to). I am spoilt for choice with regard to examples, but I wonder what investors in the "SocGen UK Step Down Defensive Kick-out Plan" think they own, for example.

Many fund names also send warning signals by breaching Smith's Law which states that you should never use a phrase if its opposite is so illogical that you would never say it. For example, you may find individuals who refer to "forward planning". Has anyone ever done any backward planning? At best, forward planning is tautology. How many companies say they will grow by means of "selective acquisitions"? Of course, none would say they have a policy of indiscriminate acquisitions (even though that is surely the reality in some cases).

What are we to make of the Sanlam Global Best Ideas Fund? Would anyone ever market a Worst Ideas Fund? If I were an investor with the group I might be concerned about what I was getting in any of their other funds. How about Pimco's Fundamental Advantage Fund? Would the fees perhaps be lower to attract investors into a Fundamental Disadvantage Fund?

Chapter 5

2014–2015

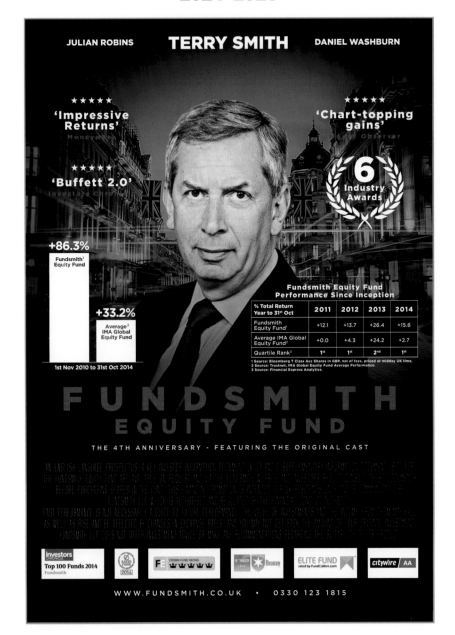

JULIAN ROBINS   **TERRY SMITH**   DANIEL WASHBURN

★★★★★
'Impressive Returns'
Moneyweek

★★★★★
'Chart-topping gains'
The Observer

★★★★★
'Buffett 2.0'
Investors Chronicle

6 Industry Awards

+86.3%
Fundsmith[1]
Equity Fund

+33.2%
Average[2]
IMA Global
Equity Fund

1st Nov 2010 to 31st Oct 2014

Fundsmith Equity Fund Performance Since Inception

% Total Return Year to 31st Oct	2011	2012	2013	2014
Fundsmith Equity Fund[1]	+12.1	+13.7	+26.4	+15.6
Average IMA Global Equity Fund[2]	+0.0	+4.3	+24.2	+2.7
Quartile Rank[3]	1st	1st	2nd	1st

1 Source: Bloomberg T Class Acc Shares in GBP, net of fees, priced at midday UK time.
2 Source: Trustnet, IMA Global Equity Fund Average Performance.
3 Source: Financial Express Analytics.

FUNDSMITH
EQUITY FUND

THE 4TH ANNIVERSARY - FEATURING THE ORIGINAL CAST

investors
Top 100 Funds 2014
Fundsmith

RATED FUND 2014

F3 CROWN FUND RATING ♛♛♛♛♛

Bronze

ELITE FUND rated by FundCalibre.com

citywire AA

WWW.FUNDSMITH.CO.UK • 0330 123 1815

Why I don't own bank shares

Financial Times, **1 November 2014**

This seems like a good week to explain why I don't own bank shares. Although it is seven years since the onset of the financial crisis, around 24–25 banks in Europe still have insufficient capital, according to the latest European Central Bank "stress tests".

I've often been asked why I won't invest in bank shares given that I was once the top-rated banking analyst in the City. The answer is that having an understanding of banks would make anyone more wary of investing in them.

One of my basic tenets is never to invest in a business which requires leverage or borrowing to make an adequate return on equity.

Most of the companies that we invest in at Fundsmith have some borrowing. But they do not require it in order to survive, and they make decent returns before the use of debt, rather than making small returns on their assets and then financing most of those assets with debt.

Banks rely on leverage to a greater extent than any other business. A 5 per cent equity to assets ratio for a bank is leverage of 19 in debt to 1 of equity.

The good news about such high leverage is that when something goes wrong, at least you go bust quickly.

Have a look below at this very simplified bank balance sheet for Lloyds Banking Group at the end of 2013:

	Liabilities (£bn)	Liabilities (%)		Assets (£bn)	Assets (%)
Equity capital	40	5	Cash	50	6
Deposits and other liabilities	807	95	Loans and other assets	797	94
Total	847	100	Total	847	100

This is not unusual. It is the normal banking model. A bank makes a small return, typically 1–2 per cent, on its total assets, but as 95 per cent of the assets are funded by depositors and bondholders, the return on equity is much higher. A return of £1 on £100 of assets is a return of 20 per cent on the £5 of equity capital.

Which is all fine – until something goes wrong. Then a loss of just 5 per cent of the value of the assets means the shareholders' equity is wiped out.

A more pernicious threat is a run on the bank. Investors had forgotten about the credit cycle until 2007, and when credit is withdrawn sometimes it is withdrawn from banks as well as their customers.

When I was analysing banks in the 1980s, it was possible – by studying the bank's accounts and regulatory returns – to gauge a bank's exposure to bad debts or credit risk, interest rates and currencies. With the advent of over-the-counter derivatives in these products, which began with interest rate swaps in the 1980s, this is no longer possible.

Someone working in the bank's treasury department may have altered all those exposures with a phone call or the click of a mouse and there is no way for investors to know. Judging by the events of the financial crisis, it is clear that a fair few bank managements were in the dark too.

All of which leads me to suggest that if you are going to own any bank shares, they should be in retail banks which simply take deposits, lend money to their own customers and make payments for them.

Such banks do exist and if I had to invest in a bank, that would be where I would look. But even those institutions are not immune to the threat which can arise from so-called systemic risk. They can be brought down by a run caused not by their own misjudgements, but by those of other banks in the system.

The fragility of banks is illustrated by a story from the 1980s, when there was a wave of nervousness in Hong Kong following the signing of the joint declaration regarding the colony's handover to China. Property prices began to collapse and banks ran up bad debts as a result.

During this febrile period, a queue of people waited for a bus. It started to rain, and the queue moved across the pavement to shelter under the cover of a canopy on a building, which happened to house a branch of a local family-controlled bank. Passers-by, seeing the queue, concluded that there was a problem with the bank. Rumours of a run spread rapidly and by the following day, the bank was besieged by depositors demanding to withdraw their savings.

Is this the next Tesco?

The Telegraph, 29 November 2014

I have been reading Warren Buffett's annual chairman's letter to the shareholders of Berkshire Hathaway for more than 30 years. But he's been having a bumpy ride lately.

Probably most conspicuous was his admission of a "huge mistake" in buying shares in Tesco. He sold part of his stake in Berkshire's only significant investment in a British company at a loss after Tesco's string of disasters.

But it is another stake purchased by Mr Buffett that is also going badly which interests me currently. In 2011 Berkshire bought a large number of shares in IBM and is now the largest shareholder, owning 7pc of the company.

IBM recently abandoned its 2015 profit target of $20 per share, having made only $10.76 in the first three quarters of this year. Its share price fell as a result to a current $162, against a high for the year of nearly $200 and an average price for Berkshire's holding of $170 per share.

By coincidence, when Mr Buffett was buying Berkshire's stake in IBM, we were looking at it for the Fundsmith Equity Fund and rejected it. Why?

The computer services giant had just delivered its "IBM 2015 Roadmap" in May 2010 via a PowerPoint presentation. My defensive instincts are immediately aroused when someone uses the term "roadmap" unless they are in a motor vehicle. "Plan" is a perfectly good and much less pretentious term.

This "roadmap" was intended to show how IBM would grow its 2010 profits of $11.52 per share to $20 by 2015.

Quite why any other investor should be impressed with this goal, even if IBM could achieve it, is beyond me.

But it is particularly curious that Mr Buffett might have been impressed given that he wrote in his 1979 chairman's letter: "The primary test of managerial economic performance is the achievement of a high earnings rate on equity capital employed (without undue leverage, accounting gimmickry, etc.) and *not the achievement of consistent gains in earnings per share.*" (Emphasis added.)

He seems to have overlooked his own advice in this case, as well as with Tesco.

Just to add to our sense of unease, the IBM "roadmap" described a number of "bridges" to growth in earnings per share. There was me thinking that a bridge was a structure that crosses a physical obstacle.

The "bridges" ("source" is a good word unless you are a civil engineer) for this "roadmapped" growth were roughly 40pc revenue growth, although this included acquisitions; 30pc "operating leverage" (cost-cutting or productivity gains in English); and 30pc share "buy-backs", where a company uses its cash to buy its own shares, reducing the number in issue.

Acquisitions, cost-cutting and share buy-backs are not a particularly high-quality source of growth. The cost-cutting and share buy-backs are certainly finite – you can't cut costs and shrink your business to growth, other than growth in earnings per share, which Mr Buffett had already correctly rejected as a useful measure of value creation or performance.

And how can you know you will make acquisitions, and doesn't price come into it?

The share buy-back "bridge" was particularly worrying. The slides show it as $50bn of planned share repurchases. How could anyone be sure that they will repurchase shares over the coming years, let alone such a vast quantity? After all, what will the share price be? If the shares are trading above their intrinsic value, a share repurchase will destroy value, other than for those shareholders who exit by taking the opportunity to sell.

Yet when he disclosed Berkshire's stake in IBM, Mr Buffett said: "I don't know of any large company that really has been as specific on what they intend to do and how they intend to do it as IBM." So he was clearly impressed by the "roadmap".

Since IBM's abandonment of its "roadmap" target for earnings per share, much has been made in articles and blogs of Mr Buffett's sanguine view of IBM's share price performance over the years of this proposed buy-back programme.

In his 2011 chairman's letter he wrote: "We should wish for IBM's stock price to languish throughout the five years [of the proposed buy-back programme]. The logic is simple: if you are going to be a net buyer of stocks in the future, either directly with your own money or indirectly (through your ownership of a company that is repurchasing shares), you are hurt when stocks rise. You benefit when stocks swoon."

This has led commentators to suggest that Mr Buffett must be cheering the drop in the IBM share price. However, there are probably a few useful words of qualification that he should have added to his views on IBM's share price and stock buy-backs. They are: "But of course it depends on the reason why the share price falls."

If the shares fall because the company's prospects have deteriorated and so has their intrinsic worth, pressing on with share buy-backs may just be a waste of money – money that belongs to Berkshire and other remaining shareholders.

Given that this is exactly what appears to have happened, I suspect that the sound which can be heard from Omaha is not the cheering that some commentators have suggested but something reminiscent of an Edvard Munch painting.

Let's all do the corporate hokey-cokey

Financial Times, 5 December 2014

There seems to have been an outbreak of the hokey-cokey participation dance song among companies lately. You know, the one where you put your right hand in, take your right hand out, shake it all about and so on.

The most prominent tendency lately seems to be to split companies into smaller enterprises, predominantly in the US but also closer to home. Even in the limited number of sectors and companies in which Fundsmith seeks to invest, there has been a rush to demerge. Just this week, Unilever announced the spin-off of its spreads business, but we have also seen:

- ADP, the payroll company, spin off its car dealership software business CDK

- eBay's announcement that it will separate its Marketplaces and PayPal businesses

- Kimberly-Clark, the tissue and nappy manufacturer, planning to spin off its healthcare business

- Procter & Gamble announcing its intention to spin off its Duracell battery business and then selling it to Warren Buffett's Berkshire Hathaway

- Reckitt Benckiser's decision to float its pharmaceutical business, to be called Indivior

And just to maintain the symmetry of the song, Coca-Cola is going through one of its periodic volte-faces on whether it is good or bad for it to own its bottlers by buying back stakes in them, many of which it had previously sold. It seems that sometimes not owning bottlers is good because it is a capital-intensive, low-return business. At other times, it is essential to own them in order to control distribution. Coke is so bipolar on this issue that it could perform the corporate M&A hokey-cokey all on its own.

In some cases, the urge to demerge seems to result from the conclusion that the company had two or more completely different businesses which did not produce any synergies and might have better futures and/or higher valuations apart from each other. One might wonder why this thought did not occur to anyone when the businesses were being acquired. Part of the answer lies in so-called shareholder activism.

Activism can take many forms and mean different things but often it involves a shareholder buying a stake in a company and then agitating for change, either via the media or through corporate governance channels.

Sometimes that change does not involve separating a company into smaller component businesses, but rather it aims to get the company to put itself up for sale. We saw this in 2011 when veteran US activist Carl Icahn made a bid for Clorox, the US household cleaning products company, in an effort to get them to sell themselves. More recently we have seen an activist make a public appeal to the board of InterContinental Hotels to put the company up for sale.

Activism definitely has a role in promoting shareholders' interests but too often it involves an attempt by the activist to get the company to do a deal which will generate some attention among the analytical community and so enable the activist to sell its stake at a profit. All very exciting, but not of much use to long-term shareholders like us who are left with holdings in fragmented businesses, often with new management teams and strained balance sheets. Then there are the huge frictional costs of separation fees to investment bankers, lawyers, accountants and others – followed by financial statements that contain so many adjustments that they border on the incomprehensible.

But sometimes seemingly frenetic merger and demerger activity is dreamt up by the management of the company all by itself. A classic case is Mondelez. It is the product of Kraft's controversial takeover of Cadbury in 2010, which was followed just two years later by the demerger of Kraft and Mondelez which consisted of Cadbury plus Kraft's snack businesses. Hardly any analysts queried why it was a good idea to demerge two businesses which it had only combined two years previously, and if you can follow the logic in all of this you are ahead of me.

The result of Kraft's hyperactivity was that the 2013 results for Mondelez – the first post demerger – contained 19 schedules of adjustments and reconciliations to its reported numbers. This legerdemain had not ceased by the first quarter of 2014, when it gave 11 adjustments, magically turning reported growth of operating profits from 1.1 per cent to 15.8 per cent. And for my next trick...

There have of course been the usual restructuring programmes and integration programmes, and the Hokey Cokey activity has not slackened with the announcement this year that Mondelez is now spinning out its coffee business into a joint venture with D.E. Master Blenders called Jacobs Douwe Egberts.

At least all this is bullish for investment bankers' bonuses.

What exactly do we mean by "shareholder value"?

Financial Times, 9 January 2015

As an investor you will probably have encountered two terms which have the word "shareholder" in common: shareholder value and activist shareholder.

Just before the end of last year we were contacted by an activist investor who has a stake in one of our portfolio companies to discuss a set of proposals. They basically amounted to a demand that the company should seek to sell itself to one of its competitors to "create additional shareholder value".

This set me thinking again about the nature of shareholder value, and indeed activism. In this and a subsequent article, I'll attempt to explain what I think these terms really mean and how they fit into the world of investment.

Company managers, fund managers and activists investors often say they are committed to generating or releasing shareholder value without ever spelling out precisely what that means. For me, it is simply determining whether or not a company is creating additional wealth for its ultimate owners, and whether its managers are acting appropriately to achieve this. I'm not sure this is everyone's definition, though. Latterly, I have come to wonder whether this concept has come to be misused, like so many others in finance.

Put simply, my definition of value creation is when a company delivers returns that are above the cost of the capital used to generate them. Companies are in essence just like us. If you borrow money at a cost of 10 per cent a year and invest it at a return of 5 per cent a year, you will become poorer. If you invest it at a return of 20 per cent a year, you will become richer.

Similarly, companies which consistently make returns above their cost of capital become more valuable and vice versa. A company that can sustain a return on capital above its cost of capital creates value for its shareholders, who should want it to retain at least part of its profits to reinvest at these attractive rates of return rather than handing them all over as dividends or using them to buy back shares.

I define returns as the "return on capital employed" or ROCE. That is fairly easily determined from company accounts; it's basically operating cash flow divided by the sum of shareholders' equity and net debt.

Determining what the cost of capital is for a company is rather more difficult. If you borrow money at a cost of 10 per cent in order to invest, then your cost of capital is fairly clear. A company's cost of debt capital is equally clear and can often be found in, or calculated from, the notes to its accounts. But what about the cost of its equity?

The commonest way of estimating this uses the so-called capital asset pricing model, often snappily known as "Cap-M" after its acronym. This defines the cost of equity capital as a risk-free rate, usually taken as the yield on government bonds in the same currency as the company, plus a risk premium. This premium is observed over time from the actual return that equities deliver relative to the bonds that form the risk-free rate.

If I haven't lost your attention with that last paragraph, I'd be amazed. And therein lies one of the problems: a company's cost of capital is not easy to define and can only ever be an estimate.

These problems have been compounded more recently because of the financial crisis. This has led some investors to query whether government bonds are truly risk-free, while ultra-low official interest rates, quantitative easing and a lack of inflation have sent bond yields down to record lows and even into negative territory.

Perhaps because cost of capital is not straightforward to define or compute, the most commonly accepted means of measuring value creation is growth in earnings per share (EPS), which is just the profits net of tax divided by the number of shares in issue. What could be simpler to calculate? Not much – which is probably why so much importance is attached to this simplistic measure of performance and its related valuation metric, the price/earnings ratio. Look through any analyst's research and you'll find dozens of references to them, often on the front page.

Simple they may be, but EPS and p/e ratios suffer from some serious flaws. The most important is that they take no account of the capital employed or the returns made on it. As the Tesco example shows, it is perfectly possible for a company to generate rising EPS at the same time as it is employing increasing amounts of capital at falling and inadequate rates of return. In other words, a company can be busy destroying shareholder value even as it increases its earnings.

So I'm sticking with ROCE as my preferred measure of value creation. But of course neither ROCE nor EPS is the same as making the share price go up. This, I suspect, is an even more common definition of shareholder value creation, especially among activist investors, of which more in the next column.

Shareholder value is an outcome, not an objective

Financial Times, **6 February 2015**

In the first article of this two-part series I explained how I define the term shareholder value: whether or not a company is able to generate a sustained return on capital employed ("ROCE") above its cost of capital. This time I want to link that definition with shareholder activism.

When an activist shareholder becomes involved in a company, the modus operandi is often something like this:

1. Acquire a stake in the company, usually via on-market purchases;

2. Campaign noisily for change, which can entail the company trying to sell itself to an acquirer, splitting itself into a number of listed entities for each of its activities, taking on more debt, buying back its own shares, or some combination of these;

3. The share price rises as a result of excitement about this activity, which it is claimed will "create shareholder value" and benefit all investors;

4. Sell the shares at a profit.

Nothing wrong with that, you might think, and certainly not from the point of view of the activist. But there is plenty wrong for those of us who are long-term investors and actually want to own the shares to gain from their ability to compound in value over time. We are often left trying to make sense of fragmented businesses, new management teams, higher leverage, the costs of separation or integration and financial statements which are rendered incomprehensible by many adjustments.

This particular problem of activism comes from confusing creating shareholder value with making the share price go up. One should lead to the other, but when short-term share price movements become the main objective, as they clearly are with many activists, the inevitable by-product is future problems for the business and its long-term shareholders.

You might conclude from this that the main target of my criticism is activists who pursue corporate action to promote short-term share price gains. But there are plenty of pitfalls for exponents of shareholder value, including those who embrace my own view on how to measure its creation.

Too often, the measures of shareholder value creation become the objectives of management. ROCE is after all only a financial ratio. In order to improve it, executives focus on getting the numerator to rise or reducing the denominator, or both.

The numerator is usually taken as operating profit, which may be increased by raising prices (which may lose market share and build a platform for competitors), cutting costs (which is not a likely source of growth), and cutting research, product development and marketing spend (to the long-term detriment of the company).

When it comes to the denominator, managers usually look to reduce the capital employed by "de-equitising" the business, using debt to buy back shares.

But if the pursuit of improving shareholder value in the form of high ROCE can lead to problems, they are nothing compared to those which can arise when growth in earnings per share is the target. A fixation on earnings per share (EPS) is one factor behind the mania which has developed for share buybacks. In an era of zero interest rates, every buyback which reduces cash or increases debt can be claimed to be "accretive to EPS". Sadly, it doesn't actually make the shrunken share base any more valuable.

When it comes to misconceived actions which aim to boost shareholder value metrics, Stanley Druckenmiller, the legendary hedge fund manager, has described IBM as a "poster child".

Last year, IBM abandoned its 2015 EPS target of $20 per share, having made only $10.76 in the first three quarters of 2014. The computer services business had delivered its "IBM 2015 Roadmap" in May 2010, purporting to show how IBM would increase its 2010 EPS of $11.52 per share to $20 by 2015.

Quite why any other investor should be impressed with this goal, even if IBM could achieve it, is beyond me. As I never tire of reminding people, EPS takes no account of the capital required to generate it, or the return on that capital.

The IBM "roadmap" described a number of "bridges" to growth in EPS. Roughly 40 per cent was to come from revenue growth, although this included acquisitions; 30 per cent "operating leverage" (cost cutting, in English); and 30 per cent from share "buybacks".

Acquisitions, cost- cutting and share buybacks are not a particularly high-quality source of growth. The cost-cutting and share buybacks are certainly finite – you can't shrink your business to growth.

The outcome for IBM has been inevitable, and not good. Investors and executives need to realise that the creation of shareholder value is an outcome – not an objective.

Why you should invest in good companies

Charles Stanley Direct, 7 February 2015

In order to understand why you should seek to invest in good companies, you first need to define what a good company is. In my view, a good company is one which creates value for its shareholders by making a high return on capital – significantly above its cost of capital – across the business and economic cycle.

Several points arise from that statement. Firstly, what is return on capital? It is usually measured by the operating profit of the business, divided by the capital employed, being the equity capital or shareholders' funds plus the net debt of the business, expressed as a percentage.

Secondly, what is the cost of capital? The cost of debt is relatively easy – you can find a reference to the cost of bonds a company has issued in the accounts, and if there is bank debt you can just use the interest charge divided by the average of opening and closing debt as the percentage cost. Cost of equity is trickier to ascertain and is usually taken as a so-called risk-free rate, such as the yield on government bonds in the same currency that the company operates in, plus a premium to compensate for the additional risks inherent in equity investment.

This slightly complex formula probably explains at least in part why so few investors seem to try to work this out. Too much time is wasted on spuriously accurate measures of cost of capital, which can only ever be an estimate. If in doubt, assume 10%.

Why is this important? Companies are just like us in some respects. If you borrowed money at 10% per year and invested it at 20%

a year, you would become richer. But if you invested at 5% you would become poorer. Similarly, a company which makes a return above its cost of capital becomes more valuable – it creates value for its shareholders – and vice versa.

But don't all companies create value for their shareholders? Sadly not. There are some industries which are prone to make returns below their cost of capital much or all of the time, such as the airline industry which has probably not created value for shareholders throughout most of its existence.

Surely if a whole industry just keeps destroying value, why would anyone invest in it? It seems hope springs eternal for some investors. They invest in companies which do not make adequate returns and so destroy value because they hope they will change – that a change of management, an upturn in the business cycle, a takeover or industry consolidation will alter this fundamentally poor characteristic.

Of course it rarely does, but that's not the only problem. Such events are not only rare and difficult to forecast, but whilst fund managers wait for their investments in bad companies to come good, they steadily erode value by the equivalent of borrowing money from you the shareholder and investing it at an inadequate rate of return.

Conversely, when you own shares in a good company, you can be sure that its value will rise over time.

Three steps to heaven

Fidelity, 27 February 2015

"Three Steps to Heaven" was a posthumous No. 1 hit by Eddie Cochran for which Showaddywaddy did a cover version. At Fundsmith it's the foundation of our investment process for the Fundsmith Equity Fund:

1. Invest in good companies

2. Don't overpay

3. Do nothing

1. A good company is one which creates value for its shareholders by making a high return on capital – significantly above its cost of capital – across the business and economic cycle.

   What is return on capital? It is usually measured by the operating profit of the business, divided by the capital employed, expressed as a percentage.

   What is the cost of capital? The cost of debt is relatively easy – you can find a reference to the cost of bonds in the accounts and if there is bank debt you can just use the interest charge divided by the average of opening and closing debt as the percentage cost. Cost of equity is trickier to ascertain and is usually taken as a so-called risk-free rate, such as the yield on government bonds in the same currency that the company operates in, plus a risk premium to compensate for the additional risks inherent in equity investment. This slightly complex formula probably explains at least in part why so few investors seem to try to work this out.

Why is this important? Companies are just like us in some respects. If you borrowed money at 10% per annum and invested it at a 20% per annum return, you would become richer. But if you invested at 5% per annum, you would become poorer. Similarly, a company which makes a return above its cost of capital becomes more valuable – it creates value for its shareholders – and vice versa.

But don't all companies create value for their shareholders? Sadly not. There are some industries which are prone to make returns below their cost of capital much or all of the time, such as the airline industry which has probably not created value for shareholders throughout most of its existence.

But surely if a whole industry just keeps destroying value, why would anyone invest in it? Fund managers invest in companies which do not make adequate returns and so destroy value because they hope they will change – that a change of management, an upturn in the business cycle, a takeover or industry consolidation will alter this fundamentally poor characteristic. Whilst fund managers wait for their investments in bad companies to come good, they steadily erode value by the equivalent of borrowing money from you the shareholder and investing it at an inadequate rate of return.

When you own shares in a good company, you can be sure that its value will rise over time.

2. Don't overpay. The secret of investment may be to buy low and sell high, but if you are buying shares in good companies, it doesn't matter if you forget the second bit. If you are going to own a portfolio of good companies with high returns which compound in value over time, you can't play "greater fool theory" in which you knowingly overpay for the shares hoping that a greater fool will buy them off you at an even more egregious valuation, as you intend to hold onto them. Which leads to:

3. Do nothing. In many ways the most difficult part of the strategy. Fund managers often seem to act as though they are paid by investors for activity when in fact they are paid for their results. And those results are generally enhanced by masterly inactivity as dealing activity costs money in terms of commissions, bid-offer spreads, and stamp duty on UK shares.

Where's the beef? McDonald's uncertain recovery

Financial Times, **22 May 2015**

Where's the beef? is a catchphrase in the US. It originated as an advertising slogan for the fast-food chain Wendy's in a TV commercial in 1984. Since then it has become an all-purpose phrase questioning the substance of an idea, event or product. It strikes me as relevant to the current predicament of McDonald's.

McDonald's, the world's largest fast-food operator, is experiencing serious problems. Global same-store sales have now been down for four consecutive quarters and six of the past nine quarters.

US same-store sales have now been down for six consecutive quarters. European same-store sales have been down for four consecutive quarters and for seven out of the past 10 quarters, and you shouldn't ask about what is happening to McDonald's Japanese sales if you are squeamish.

Perhaps even worse is the fact that the number of customers visiting McDonald's in the US fell 1.6 per cent in 2013 and then 4.1 per cent in 2014. The European guest count fell 1.5 per cent in 2013 and then 2.2 per cent in 2014.

Nor are things any better in the developing world. Same-store sales in Asia-Pacific, the Middle East and Africa have been down for eight of the last 10 quarters and the guest count fell 3.8 per cent in 2013 and 4.7 per cent in 2014.

In other words, fewer people are going to McDonald's and the rate of decline is accelerating.

Some commentators would have you believe that the problem rests with the entire sector, for which they use the pejorative term "junk food". Yet Domino's Pizza reported results for its first quarter ended March 2015 with US same-store sales up by 14.5 per cent, and this is not an isolated example.

Nor can McDonald's blame the economy: the company managed 3.8 per cent same-store growth in 2009 and 6.9 per cent in 2008. Comparable global sales grew in every month in 2008 and 2009.

The fact is, there is something fundamentally wrong with McDonald's rather than the whole fast-food sector. It affects all regions of its operation and it is getting worse.

At least McDonald's has figured out that it has a problem. The result is a new chief executive, Steve Easterbrook, who ran the relatively successful UK operations, and the obligatory "turnround plan" launched at an investor conference.

My misgivings about this plan began with the news release which preceded the conference. It said the new chief executive identified the company's priorities as threefold: "driving operational growth, returning excitement to our brand and unlocking financial value". It continued, "the first critical step of our operational growth-led plan is to strengthen our effectiveness and efficiency and drive faster and more customer-led decisions". I'm not sure I know what this means, but what will he do to achieve it?

Restructure the business, of course, into four new segments. As well as the US, the business will have three other segments – "international lead markets", "high growth markets" and "foundational markets". How rearranging the reporting segmentation will help is beyond me – a phrase about the rearrangement of the deck chairs on the Titanic springs to mind.

Note that the word "food" was entirely absent from the release and the word "burger" was only mentioned once, as in "burger company".

Language which felt like it had been lifted from a management consultancy lexicon continued in the chief executive's presentation: "As we turn around our critical markets, we will create strategies which leverage our scale and competing power, bring disruptions to life and sharp brands on the move. We will also seek to be more progressive around our social purpose in order to deepen our relationships with communities on the issues that matter to them." Note, still no mention of the food.

I think that the first thing McDonald's needs to address is whether its target customers like the food it sells, and if not, figure out why this is and what it can do about it. Domino's Pizza did this in 2009 when it made a very public mea culpa about the quality of its pizzas, publishing some damning findings from a customer survey along the lines of "the cardboard box tastes better than the pizzas". This is the sort of action you only take if you intend to change and Domino's has been reaping the benefits since.

But I don't think we should solely blame McDonald's management for this lack of focus on the one thing that matters more than any other – the food. The analytical and investment community must share the blame. To illustrate why, here are the first three questions from analysts in the Q&A session following the chief executive's presentation:

1. The first questioner asked whether the increase in the percentage of franchised restaurants, which McDonald's is planning, would be dilutive or accretive to earnings per share ("EPS").

2. The second questioner suggested that the higher franchised percentage should enable the company to support a higher level of debt.

3. The third question was on whether the company had considered an OpCo-PropCo structure in which a company's properties are held in a "PropCo" and leased to the Operating Company or "OpCo" with the PropCo then usually sold to "unlock the value" in the company's real estate.

In other words, all these analysts seemed to be interested in was financial engineering. They do not seem to realise that without a business selling something which customers want, no amount of financial wizardry will create lasting value. But faced with this obsession with financial legerdemain among the analysts, you can hardly blame the management for sharing some of the same focus.

If you are thinking of investing in McDonald's or any other potential "turnround" situation, I suggest you hold back until you encounter a CEO who talks about the need to improve the company's product or service in a basic manner. Someone who can answer the question, "Where's the beef?"

Fundsmith

What investors can learn from Alex Bird's 500 winning bets at the races

The Telegraph, 12 June 2015

"They think it's all over." Commentator Kenneth Wolstenholme's remark at the end of the 1966 World Cup Final has passed into popular culture as a widely used expression. But I am amazed how little investors learn from the world of sport, which has a lot to teach us.

In managing the Fundsmith Equity Fund, we seek to invest in companies that have a long history of success in a few sectors such as consumer staples, medical equipment and franchising.

People often say to us: "Oh, you try to pick winners." The reality is that we don't seek to predict who will win, but rather to bet on a company that has already won.

To explain what we seek to do, I would turn to the world of horse racing. As a professional gambler, Alex Bird made a fortune betting on photo finishes. You can read about it in his autobiography, *Alex Bird: The Life and Secrets of a Professional Punter.*

In Bird's day, photo finishes were not digital and it took several minutes to develop the film and view the outcome, during which time bookmakers continued laying odds on the outcome.

Bird realised that they were breaking one of the fundamental rules of bookmaking – never make odds on an event that has already occurred, as someone who knows the outcome can take you to the cleaners.

Allegedly, bookmakers in the vicinity of St James's Palace learnt this the hard way when they laid odds on the name of royal babies while the Queen Mother, who liked a bet, was still alive.

Bird noticed that when horses crossed the line together, the horse on the far side often appeared to have won. What he had figured out was "parallax": the difference in the apparent position of an object viewed along two different lines of sight.

He discovered a simple technique to exploit this. By standing as near to the winning post as possible, closing one eye and creating an imaginary line across the track at the finishing line, he could tell which horse had actually won. Using this simple system for the next 20 years he made himself a fortune, with a reported 500 consecutive successful bets.

This can happen in the financial world. When Warren Buffett announced that after a career investing only in the US he had bought a British share for the first time, the bookmakers made odds on which share it was. This was dangerous given that a number of intermediaries, such as Berkshire Hathaway's brokers, already knew.

What has all this got to do with investment? At Fundsmith we do not seek to pick winners in the sense that most punters do, which is studying form, viewing the horses in the ring and then betting.

We seek to emulate Alex Bird – we wait until we know who has won and then wait for the bookmakers to offer us odds against them winning. In our case, these are not bookmakers in the sense of a racecourse; we are talking about the market mispricing shares.

There are some companies where we do not need to speculate on whether they have won in the sense of being successful and dominating certain product categories. Nestlé is the world's largest food and beverage company and has been in business for 148 years with only one loss. Colgate-Palmolive has 45pc of the world market for toothpaste and 35pc for toothbrushes. It is also the leader in liquid soap and third in pet food. We simply need to wait until the market misprices these shares in order to get our chance to bet on a certain winner.

This can happen for many reasons, for example when a panic occurs such as the whole market experienced in 2008–2009. Or it can come about because investors sensing recovery dump known winners and turn to the shares that rise most in such circumstances, such as cyclicals, financials, recovery stocks and highly indebted companies.

It may entail particular concerns about the product, such as cola drinks or micro beads in toothpaste, or a milk powder safety scare. Or currency moves such as the recent rise in the Swiss franc, which sent Nestlé's shares down by more than 10pc even though 98pc of its business is outside Switzerland.

Situations such as these can all provide chances to invest by betting on a certain winner if they drive the valuation to a level which does not reflect these companies' sustainable returns.

What investors can learn from Sir Alex Ferguson's success

The Telegraph, **19 June 2015**

Investors can learn a lot from the world of sport. Last week I looked at how the professional punter Alex Bird made a fortune betting on horse races after the race was over.

The moral of his story: don't try to predict which horse will win, but find a way to bet on the horse that has already won. An important element of success in sports, and in investment, is narrowing the chance of success.

Another good example comes from football. Research by the United States Sports Academy found that more than 90pc of goals in the matches studied were scored from inside the penalty area. Faced with these statistics, any sensible player would stop shooting from outside the area.

How does this apply to the world of investment? Many investors spend their time trying to predict the next big winner in a sector, particularly in technology, despite the difficulty of forecasting developments in this area.

The table shows the top 10 software companies from just over 30 years ago. All bar one have more or less ceased to exist. Clearly trying to predict a long-term winner in the software sector is extremely difficult, even if you start with those that are already leading. What must the odds be like if you are backing start-ups and early-stage investments?

Top 10 software companies in 1984	
1	Microsoft
2	VisiCorp
3	DRI
4	Micropro
5	Lotus
6	Ashton-Tate
7	Peachtree
8	SPC
9	CAR/Sorcim
10	Perfect

Source: Fundsmith

This question is answered in part if you look at the results of clinical trials in the biotechnology and pharmaceutical sector.

Clinical trials involving new drugs are commonly classified into four phases: zero, one, two and three. Only if a drug passes all four phases will it usually be approved by the national regulatory authority for use in the general population.

A study by KMR Group published in 2012 used data on drug successes and failures between 2007 and 2011 submitted by 13 of the world's largest pharmaceutical firms. It found that 97pc of drugs in preclinical tests never made it, and neither did 95pc of the molecules in phase one clinical trials or 88pc of molecules in phase two. Not until phase three did prospects get much better – of the ones that made it that far, 54pc were approved.

The odds of a drug at the preclinical stage making it all the way are one in 10,000 (if you are interested in the maths, the calculation is $(1-0.97) \times (1-0.95) \times (1-0.88) \times (1-0.46) = 0.0001$). Trying to pick winners in the early stages of drug trials by investing in biotech companies is clearly a full-contact sport.

You can also learn something about companies' prospects from changes of manager, just as you can with sports teams.

What did you expect the outcome to be when Sir Alex Ferguson retired as manager of Manchester United after 27 years, a time in which the club won 13 Premier League titles, five FA Cups, four League Cups, 10 Community Shields, two UEFA Champions Leagues, the UEFA Super Cup, the Intercontinental Cup, and the FIFA Club World Cup?

It is hard not to see his short-lived successor, David Moyes, as the recipient of a so-called "hospital pass". In his brief reign of less than a year, Manchester United won only the Community Shield.

There are parallels in the retirement of Sir Terry Leahy as chief executive of Tesco. When Sir Terry stepped down, laden with accolades, after 14 years, he was replaced by Philip Clarke, who lasted just three years – a period strewn with profit warnings, food contamination scares and an accounting scandal.

I am not suggesting that any of this was Mr Clarke's fault. In my view, the root of the problem lay in the Leahy years, but came to light only after the charismatic leader had left.

Similarly, it wasn't all that hard to predict the outcome when Jim Skinner, the chief executive who was credited with turning McDonald's fortunes around, left in 2012 after eight years at the helm during which he was named as "chief executive of the year". His successor, Don Thompson, lasted the obligatory three years before admitting defeat.

The point of this is not who is to blame for the slide in the fortunes of McDonald's, Manchester United or Tesco, but that investors should be wary when a long-standing and highly successful chief executive leaves a business, just as football fans are.

As an old saying goes: acorns do not flourish under mighty oaks.

Bond proxies: can you afford not to own them?

Financial Times, 26 June 2015

"It's far better to buy a wonderful company at a fair price than a fair company at a wonderful price," Warren Buffett once said. I agree with Mr Buffett's description of a good company. To quote from his 1979 annual chairman's letter: "The primary test of managerial economic performance is the achievement of a high earnings rate on equity capital employed (without undue leverage, accounting gimmickry, etc.) and not the achievement of consistent gains in earnings per share."

What Mr Buffett is describing is return on equity capital and despite this guidance more than 35 years ago from one of the world's most successful investors, his advice continues to be ignored by most. One of the objections levelled at investors who attempt to invest along the lines which Mr Buffett suggested – and I would count myself as one of them – is that the sort of companies with these characteristics may be too expensive. This concern has reached fever pitch recently, with myriad warnings about what will happen to so-called "bond proxies" when US interest rates rise. A "bond proxy" is shorthand to describe equities such as consumer staples and utilities with safe, predictable returns, but have higher yields than much of the bond market (and, crucially, yields which can grow over time).

Bond markets have experienced a bull run since the financial crisis and the onset of quantitative easing, which has seen central banks pump billions into buying their own governments' bonds, and a disinflationary environment which has led to the sister policy of zero interest rates. Faced with seemingly ever-lower yields, investors have crowded into equities in general and especially those which are considered "bond proxies". The obvious problem is what happens if – or when – interest rates rise. Bond yields then rise and those equities which have been used as bond proxies will surely fare badly. I would suggest a slightly less simplistic approach.

Let's start with the assumption that interest rates will rise. Eventually that must be true, but when and by how much is less easy to predict. The "when" has some bearing on the matter. There are a number of fine fund managers who have had their performance shredded by attempting to time this and other events. The "how much" also matters. In my view, we remain in a disinflationary environment with a mostly weak economic recovery, so the rise when it comes may not be anything like the gradient which we have come to expect from previous recoveries. Short-term interest rates may be at or close to zero and may rise, but they are of less significance in valuing bonds and equities than long-term rates, and US 30-year Treasuries already yield over 3 per cent. This yield may not budge much.

If you are worrying about bond proxy equities in this scenario, you might also like to ask yourself where you will put the money that you realise from selling them. Into cash? Good luck with your timing. Into bonds? I think not. Into other equities? Maybe, but the S&P 500 Index's price/earnings ratio is 19x, so it's not that they are obviously cheap, and most of the Index is much more heavily cyclical than the bond proxies, making it an interesting choice if you are seeking safety in a rising rate environment. One thing we can be sure of is that the stocks in the index are not of the same quality as the so-called bond proxies.

There is another quote from Mr Buffett's business partner, Charlie Munger, on this subject: "Over the long term, it's hard for a stock to earn a much better return than the business which underlies it earns. If the business earns 6 per cent on capital over 40 years and you hold it for that 40 years, you're not going to make much different than a 6 per cent return – even if you originally buy it at a huge discount. Conversely, if a business earns 18 per cent on capital over 20 or 30 years, even if you pay an expensive-looking price, you'll end up with one hell of a result."

I agree with them both about this. Let's take two examples of potential investments which you can make and hold for 40 years – from when you start work in your 20s until you retire. Company A (the bond proxy) generates a return on capital employed (ROCE) of 20 per cent per annum throughout this period. It has ample opportunities to grow and can reinvest all of its earnings each year at the same rate of return. That's the good news. The bad news is that its shares are not cheap and to buy them you have to pay four times book value. That's not all – when you come to sell them in 40 years' time, the rating has halved and you can only sell them for two times book value.

Company B (the market) earns a 10 per cent ROCE over this period and reinvests all its earnings at that rate of return. Moreover, the investors who take this option have better luck in terms of timing, as they can buy B's shares at two times book value and when they come to sell them in 40 years, they can sell them for four times book value – their rating has doubled.

So if these were the alternatives on offer for your investment career, which would you take?

Company A would produce compound returns of 18 per cent per annum and Company B 12 per cent per annum. If you plan to hold a share for the long term, the rate of return on capital it generates and can reinvest at is far more important than the rating you buy or sell at.

That's why if you are a long-term investor, you should own the high-quality bond proxies and close your ears to the siren song of those who say a rate rise will cause you problems. If you are not a long-term investor, I wonder what you are doing in the stock market at all and so will you one day.

Why bother cooking the books if no one reads them?

Financial Times, **24 September, 2015**

In August 1992, my book *Accounting for Growth* was published. It exposed how companies used accounting trickery to flatter their reported performance. Nowadays, there are brokers such as Muddy Waters and Iceberg who specialise in revealing these practices, but in 1992 such research was most unusual so it caused quite a stir.

My then employer tried to stop its publication, which of course only made people want to read it, sending it to the top of the non-fiction charts. I was fired, which sent my career off in a more entrepreneurial direction, and several of the companies named in the book got into serious difficulty or simply went bust.

A second edition was published in 1996 and I've often been asked to reprise the subject with another book.

One of the reasons I haven't is that publication of the book roughly coincided with the start of a successful campaign by the Accounting Standards Board, led by Sir David Tweedie, to stamp out many of the abuses in company accounting.

Another is that I am not sure many investors or analysts study company accounts any longer. Instead, they seem to rely upon management presentations using "adjusted", "core" or "underlying" earnings or profits.

One sector in which my Fundsmith Equity Fund does not own any stocks is pharmaceuticals. This seems to surprise some commentators, who think that drug companies would represent exactly the sort of dependable returns we seek. After all, such stocks benefit from seemingly inexorable growth in demand for healthcare, especially among the ageing populations of the developed world, and margins that are shielded from competition by patents.

One reason we don't own them is that the sector has become rated on the basis of "underlying" earnings. Beginning in about 2010, many major pharmaceutical companies started a switch to reporting what they term "core" earnings. This switch was allegedly to smooth out exceptional items from reported earnings and make trends more recognisable.

So what is excluded from earnings based on generally accepted accounting principles (GAAP) to get to "core" earnings?

1. Restructuring costs, although they seem to be a recurring item in the accounts of a number of companies. GlaxoSmithKline, for example, has not had a quarter without any since 2008.

2. "Exceptional" legal charges. Once again, given the nature of the industry involving patents, patent disputes, regulation and product liability, it seems inevitable that significant legal expenses will be a more or less constant feature of a pharmaceutical company's profit & loss (P&L) account. So it is hard to see how they are by nature exceptional.

3. Intangible asset amortisation and impairment. When pharmaceutical companies buy a drug from another company or buy another drug company – and they have been doing a lot of that – they create intangible assets that represent the amount they paid over and above the tangible or hard assets acquired. This is usually the vast majority, if not all, of the cost

and GAAP requires it to be both amortised by a charge to the profit and loss account, usually over the life of the drug patents, and written off in the event that a drug fails its trials – a not infrequent event.

Some will argue that it is acceptable to exclude these intangible charges as they are "non-cash", but doing so turns the P&L account into a hybrid of accrual accounting and cash flows. If you are interested in a company's cash flow, and you should be, the place to gauge that is in the cash flow statement, not a doctored P&L account which excludes some non-cash items. AstraZeneca, for example, has over £16bn of these intangibles on its balance sheet which would cause an annual charge of some £1.6bn, but this is not reflected in its "core" earnings.

Moreover, excluding these intangible items means that the cost of acquiring new drugs and biotech companies does not appear anywhere in these "core" earnings. In light of this, is it any surprise that the pharmaceutical sector has been on a binge of buying biotech companies, spending $80bn in 2014 alone?

All of the adjustments have one thing in common – they make the reported "core" earnings higher.

Faced with this opportunity to flatter the earnings, it is also no wonder that management incentives have been remodelled to take advantage, with some or all of management remuneration in the sector based on "core" earnings.

Unsurprisingly, since 2010 the GAAP earnings per share (EPS) in the sector have decreased significantly as a percentage of "core"

EPS – in the case of AstraZeneca from 84 per cent to just 23 per cent by 2014. In other words, as their pay has come to depend upon "core" earnings, more and more bad stuff has been excluded from the calculation.

For example, AstraZeneca reported GAAP EPS of $5.60 in 2010 but courtesy of "core" earnings this became EPS of $6.17. By 2014 the GAAP EPS of just $0.98 had become "core" EPS of $4.28.

The net result of all this is that the ratings which many pharmaceutical stocks, appear to trade on bear little resemblance to reality based on their GAAP earnings:

	GAAP PE	Core PE
AstraZeneca	69.5	15.9
GlaxoSmithKline	22.5	13.5
Novartis	22.9	18.6
Sanofi	26.8	17.2
Bristol-Myers Squibb	52.6	34.2
Eli Lilly	39.6	31.7
Pfizer	24.6	15.5

In my view, if you are an investor in pharmaceutical stocks, this should worry you a lot. If you want to know more, broker Badon Hill recently published a critical – and in my view good – research report on "Big Pharma". The irony is that in order to discover what is really going on, you do not need to be a sophisticated financial analyst. All you need to do is get the GAAP EPS number from the accounts.

Hence my view that there is no point in companies engaging in any form of accounting chicanery, when their legerdemain seems to have the entire market looking somewhere other than the accounts.

What I have learnt at Fundsmith in the past five years

Financial Times, 21 November 2015

Fundsmith, my fund management business, celebrated its fifth anniversary in the past month. What have I learnt over the past five years of running the fund?

One thing I have observed is the obsession of market commentators, investors and advisers with macroeconomics, interest rates, quantitative easing, asset allocation, regional geographic allocation, currencies, developed markets versus emerging markets — whereas they almost never talk about investing in good companies.

It seems to me that most of these subjects pose questions to which no one can reliably forecast the answers, and even if you could the connection to asset prices is tenuous at best. Take GDP growth — few things seem to obsess commentators more, yet no one has ever managed to demonstrate a positive correlation between GDP growth and stock market performance.

Invest in something good

What has continued to amaze me throughout the past five years is not just this largely pointless obsession with factors which are unknowable, largely irrelevant, or both, but how infrequently I hear fund managers or investors talk about investing in something which is good. Like a good company with good products or services, strong market share, good profitability, cash flow and product development.

I suppose I had assumed that the credit crisis might have taught them that you will struggle to make a good return from poor-quality assets. No amount of CLOs, CDOs and the other alphabet soup of structured finance managed to turn subprime loans into a good investment. When the credit cycle turned down, even the triple-A rated tranches of these instruments turned out to be triple-Z. There's a saying involving silk purses and a sow's ears which encapsulates the problem.

I am not suggesting that there is no other way of making money other than to invest in good companies, but investing in poor or even average companies presents problems. One is that over time they tend to destroy rather than create value for shareholders, so a long-term buy and hold strategy is not going to work for them.

A more active trading strategy also has its drawbacks. Apart from the drag on performance from trading costs, it is evident from the performance of most funds that very few active managers are sufficiently skilled to buy shares in poor companies when their performance and share prices are depressed, and then sell them close to their cyclical peak.

Another obsession I have been surprised about is that with "cheap" shares. I have been asked whether a share is cheap many more times than I have been asked whether the company is a good business.

This obsession often manifests itself in the critique of our strategy which goes something like, "These companies may be high-quality, but the shares are too expensively rated." This is almost certain to be true, as from time to time the share prices are sure to decline, but it misses the point. If you are a long-term investor, owning shares in a good company is a much larger determinant of your investment performance than whether the shares were cheap when you bought them.

Ignore the siren song

A fairly obvious lesson, but one I have re-learnt, is to stick to your guns and ignore popular opinion. I lost count of the number of times I was asked why we didn't own Tesco shares, or was told that I had to own Tesco shares when our analysis showed quite clearly that its earnings-per-share growth had been achieved at the expense of returns on capital. In fact, its return on capital had deteriorated in a manner which pointed to serious problems in Tesco's new investment in areas such as China and California.

Similarly, it is important to ignore the siren song of those who have views on stocks which you hold, particularly if they are based on prejudices about their products. I also lost count of the number of comments I read about how Microsoft was finished as it "wasn't Apple". This included one investor who rang us to ask if we had seen the quarterly numbers from Microsoft which were not good. (It was tempting to respond saying No, of course we had not seen the quarterly results for one of our largest holdings and thank him for pointing this revelation out to us.)

He said we would face questions at our AGM if we still held the stock then. It was of course just one quarter and the stock more or less doubled in price after that. Sadly no question was raised at the AGM.

Stick to the facts

Another of my observations is that impressions about stocks are often formed erroneously because people do not check the simplest facts. Sometimes they simply relate to the wrong company.

We topped up our stake in Del Monte, a processed food and pet food business, on some share price weakness which resulted when a news service carried an article that dock workers in Galveston had gone on strike and so had stopped Del Monte's ships being unloaded. The company it was actually referring to was Del Monte Fresh Foods, which imports tropical fruits like bananas and pineapples, not the one we were invested in. Or the client who contacted us to say how concerned he was about our large holding in Domino's Pizza since the chief executive and chief financial officer had left. They had left the UK company, but we owned the US master franchiser.

I would be hard pressed to name the least well understood subject in investment given the wide choice available, but I suspect that currencies is among the leaders. Over the past five years I have heard lots of people talk or ask about the impact of currencies in a manner which betrays a complete lack of understanding of the subject. The commonest question or assumption about our fund is the impact of the US dollar, since the majority of the companies we have owned since inception are headquartered and listed in the US.

This makes little or no sense. A company's currency exposure is not determined by where it is headquartered, listed or which currency it denominates its accounts in. Yet this does not seem to stop people assuming that it does and making statements about the exposure of our fund to the US dollar, based on where the companies are listed.

We own one company which is headquartered and listed in the US, but which has no revenues there at all. Clearly this assumption would not work very well for that company, any more than it would work for the UK listed company we own which has the US as its biggest market and which, perhaps unsurprisingly, reports its accounts in US dollars.

Nor could we understand the reasoning of the commentators who wrote that our holding in Nestlé had benefited from the rise in the Swiss franc. How? Ninety-eight per cent of Nestlé's revenues are outside Switzerland. It may be headquartered and listed in Switzerland and report in Swiss francs, but the fact is that a company's currency exposure is mainly determined by where it does business. In Nestlé's case the Indian rupee is a bigger exposure than the Swiss franc.

Does anyone read accounts?

I have also discovered that hardly anyone reads company accounts any more. Instead they rely upon management presentations of figures which often present "underlying", "core" or "adjusted" numbers. Not coincidentally, the adjustments to get to the core or underlying numbers almost always seem to remove negative items. Reading the actual accounts bypasses this accounting legerdemain.

We have also discovered mistakes in accounts which no one else seems to have noticed. Like the $1.8bn mistake in the IBM cash flow. This alone did not prevent us investing in IBM, but it helped to support our conclusion that hardly anyone reads its accounts thoroughly.

Don't sell good companies

I have also learnt that selling a stake in a good company is almost always a mistake. Take Sigma-Aldrich, a US chemical company based in St Louis. It supplies pots of chemicals to scientists around the world who use them in tests and experiments. Its financial performance fitted our criteria, as did its operational characteristics — supplying 170,000 products to more than a million customers at an average price of $400 per product. It fitted our mantra of making its money from a large number of everyday repeat transactions, as well as having a base of loyal scientists who relied on its service.

It was a predictable company of exactly the type we seek. That was until it was revealed that it was trying to acquire Life Technologies, a much larger company which supplies lab equipment. Given the execution risk involved, we sold our stake. As it happens, Sigma-Aldrich did not acquire Life Technologies as it was outbid. But having gone public on its willingness to combine with another business, it was in no position to defend its independence and succumbed to a bid itself from Merck at a price about 40 per cent above the price we had sold at.

Selling good companies is rarely a good move. The good news is that we don't do it very often.

Our best share

Domino's Pizza Inc, with a return of over 600 per cent from the initial stake purchased on the day the fund opened. What might we learn from this?

- People often assume that for an investment to make a high return it must be esoteric, obscure, difficult to understand and undiscovered by other investors. On the contrary — the best investments are often the most obvious.

- Run your winners. Too often investors talk about "taking a profit". If you have a profit on an investment it might be an indication that you own a share in a business which is worth holding on to. Conversely, we are all prone to run our losers, hoping they will get back to what we paid for them. Gardeners nurture flowers and pull up weeds, not the other way around.

- Domino's is a franchiser. If you regard a high return on capital as the most important sign of a good business, few are better than businesses which operate through franchises, as most of the capital is supplied by them. The franchiser get a royalty from revenues generated by other people's capital.

- Domino's has focused on the most important item for success in its sector - the food. This is in sharp contrast to other fast food providers like McDonald's which are struggling.

- Domino's is mostly a delivery business. This means that it can operate from cheaper premises in secondary locations, and so cut the capital required to operate compared with fast food operators who need high street restaurant premises.

- Domino's was owned by Bain Capital. Like a lot of private equity firms, Bain leveraged up the business by taking on debt to pay themselves a dividend before IPO, so it started life as a public company with high leverage. This can enhance equity returns. In a business which can service the debt there is a transfer of value to the equity holders as the debt is paid down and the equity is de-risked. Please note — this does NOT indicate that leverage always enhances returns.

Celebrating 5 years
of investing in decades of success

The Fundsmith Equity Fund invests in a small number of high quality, resilient, global growth companies that were founded on average in 1908, are good value and which we intend to hold for the long term.

An English language prospectus, a Key Investor Information Document (KIID) and a Supplementary Information Document (SID) for the Fundsmith Equity Fund are available on request and via the Fundsmith website and investors should consult these documents before purchasing shares in the fund. This financial promotion is intended for UK residents only and is communicated by Fundsmith LLP which is authorised and regulated by the Financial Conduct Authority.

Past performance is not necessarily a guide to future performance. The value of investments and the income from them may fall as well as rise and be affected by changes in exchange rates, and you may not get back the amount of your original investment.

Fundsmith LLP does not offer investment advice or make any recommendations regarding the suitability of its product.

% Total Return Year to 31st Oct	2015	2014	2013	2012	2011
Fundsmith Equity Fund (1)	+18.5	+15.6	+26.4	+13.7	+12.1
Investment Assoc. Global Sector (2)	+4.5	+4.2	+24.2	+4.3	+0.0
Quartile Rank (2)	1st	1st	2nd	1st	1st

(1) Source: Fund NAV, T Class Acc Shares in GBP, net of fees, priced at midday UK time. (2) Source: Financial Express Analytics, 203 Funds.

+121%
Fundsmith Equity Fund (1)

+41%
Investment Assoc. Global Sector (2)

1st Nov 2010 to 31st Oct 2015

www.fundsmith.co.uk
0330 123 1815

Fundsmith
Equity Fund

    Fidelity HARGREAVES LANSDOWN TD Direct Investing